ACRL Monograph Number 26 7-12

The Printed Book Catalogue in American Libraries: 1723-1900

by Jim Ranz Dean of Academic Affairs, University of Wyoming

American Library Association   Chicago 1964

The Library of Congress card number for the
ACRL Monograph Series is 52-4228. The card
number of this title is 64-17055.

Contents

ACKNOWLEDGMENTS

This study was originally prepared in partial fulfillment of the requirements for the degree of Doctor of Philosophy in Library Science at the University of Illinois, 1960.

In the preparation of the work, I incurred the debt of several people: Dr. Thelma Eaton, under whose supervision the study was written, for much helpful encouragement, criticism, and direction; Dr. Robert B. Downs, Dr. William V. Jackson, and the other members of my thesis committee for a careful reading of the manuscript; members of the University of Illinois Library staff for the procurement of needed materials; Mrs. Esther Kelley, for typing and proofreading the manuscript; and, finally, my wife, Delores, for immeasurable patience and understanding.

Jim Ranz

Introduction

Until 1900 the printed book catalogue was of the utmost concern to American librarians and a topic concerning which they wrote both frequently and ardently. Then for almost half a century it was superseded by the printed card catalogue. Now the printed book catalogue has reappeared, and librarians once again are discussing it in print. It is surprising, therefore, that no general and comprehensive account of the subject has ever appeared.[1] The present study undertakes to provide the historical background of the printed catalogue, bringing the story to the end of the nineteenth century, at which time the book catalogue passed into a temporary oblivion. It is to be hoped that other and, perforce, later studies will describe the increasing revival of the book catalogue which has occurred during the past ten or fifteen years.[2]

SCOPE OF STUDY

The library catalogue prepared as a guide for the reader has come quite properly to be known as the "public catalogue." In form, composition, and specific aims it has varied from one time to another and from library to library; but its basic purpose has remained unchanged—to furnish readers with an index to the library's stock of books. Through the years librarians have also found it desirable to prepare other records—shelf lists, accession registers, official catalogues, and the like—all of which have indirectly assisted the reader in his use of the library. This study is limited, however, to that catalogue prepared expressly for the reader and used directly by him—the public catalogue—and that only when in printed book form.

It should be stated explicitly that the catalogues of book dealers and publishers are excluded. Also omitted are the catalogues of personal collections unless they are readily available to all qualified readers. Included, then, are only the catalogues of those libraries which, in the words of C. C. Jewett, "are accessible—either without restriction, or upon conditions with which all can easily comply—to every person who wishes to use them for their appropriate purpose."[3]

To keep the study within manageable bounds, only the catalogues of libraries within the area of the continental United States are considered. To the extent that the printed catalogue movement transcended national boundaries, this poses an arbitrary limitation. An attempt is made in the first chapter, however, to trace briefly the development of the book catalogue prior to its introduction in America early in the eighteenth century. Throughout the remainder of the study occasional references are made to significant developments in other countries, particularly England.

Inasmuch as this is a historical study, it is based largely upon existing documentary evidence, the major portion of which concerns the larger and better-supported libraries. Literature concerning the activities of the smaller and poorer libraries is infrequently found, primarily because it was never prepared and published. As a result, this study is oriented toward what might be termed the "better cataloguing practices of the day." For this reason little attempt has been made to present in tabular or chart form quantitative evidence concerning the cataloguing practices of all libraries. The limited documentation for the smaller libraries is largely offset by the fact that the larger libraries, with their better-trained staffs and more adequate budgets, made most of the advances in cataloguing.

The study covers a period of almost two centuries. It begins early in the eighteenth century with the printing of the first library catalogue in America; it ends late in the nineteenth century with the announcement by the Library of Congress of a plan for the production of printed catalogue cards. For almost half a century afterward, the book catalogue passed into disuse. Only an occasional library was brave—or rash—enough to print one; the expense was too great, the Library of Congress printed cards too convenient.

The past decade has seen a heartening revival of the printed book catalogue. New photographic and reproductive techniques give promise of removing the only real objection to the book catalogue—the cost of its production. A host of libraries, led by the Library of Congress, King County Library of Seattle, Los Angeles County Library, and the New York State Library, are using tabulating cards in a variety of ways for the production of book

catalogues. G. K. Hall and Company of Boston is proceeding in
quite another direction—the combining of microphotography with
electrostatic printing to reproduce card catalogues in book form.
At the present time, Hall has in print the catalogues (comprising
almost 800 volumes in all) of some sixty research collections. [4]
But these movements are only beginning to unfold, and their full
history cannot as yet be told.

SOURCES

The printed catalogues themselves quite obviously provided
the most important source of documentary evidence for this study.
Approximately one thousand catalogues were examined with varying degrees of completeness. Those which made significant contributions were studied at length; their prefaces and other introductory matter were especially informative. In addition to outlin-
ing the plan of the catalogue, the prefatory material frequently included a brief history of the library, its constitution and bylaws,
and personal comments by the compiler concerning the general
problems of preparing and printing catalogues.

The annual reports of libraries furnished a second excellent
source of primary materials. They occasionally contained fuller
accounts of the circumstances surrounding the printing of catalogues than did the catalogues themselves. Also found in these annual reports was information which, by its nature, could not be included in the catalogues: for example, the reception accorded the
catalogue by readers, number of copies sold, and even the abortive
attempts to print catalogues.

Additional material, some of it of a secondary nature, was obtained from various other sources. Of considerable importance
were several articles appearing in periodicals, particularly in the
Library Journal, from 1876 to 1906 the official organ of the American Library Association. Critical reviews of printed catalogues
furnished another excellent source, especially for contemporary
opinion. Finally, histories of individual libraries supplied much
useful information.

Chapter I

The Printed Book Catalogue in Colonial America

The reader in a modern American library, thumbing matter-of-factly through a drawer of catalogue cards, would be surprised to learn that only in recent times have libraries used this means for listing the books in their collections. In fact, the card catalogue was not even introduced in libraries until after 1850 and was not used generally until after 1875. For centuries before, the form of the catalogue was a book—at first in manuscript and later, in the larger and more affluent libraries, in print.

CATALOGUING HERITAGE

When Joshua Gee began work on the first library catalogue printed in America, the Harvard College catalogue (in Latin) of 1723,[1] he had a sizable cataloguing tradition upon which to draw. On the shelves of the Harvard Library, for example, were several volumes on the art of cataloguing, as well as a number of the actual printed catalogues of English and European libraries.

Of the early writers on catalogues, Gee probably found the works of three men most helpful: Konrad Gesner, the German physician, naturalist, and bibliographer; Florian Trefler, the Benedictine monk; and Andrew Maunsell, the English bookseller. Of the three, Gesner was the pioneer. One writer has summarized his contribution by stating that "for the first time, attention was paid to the entry word."[2] Gesner's *Bibliotheca universalis*,[3] an alphabetical author listing of all known scholarly works, appeared in 1545. Three years later, he published his *Pandectarum*,[4] a subject index, which also contained his thoughts on library management.

Appearing only a decade after Gesner's works was Florian Trefler's essay on the desirability of multiple approaches within

1

a catalogue.[5] This he sought to accomplish by using a five-part
catalogue made up of an alphabetical author sequence of entries, a
classified subject sequence, a classified subject index to parts of
books, an alphabetical author index to parts of books, and a list of
books not shelved with the main collection.

The last of the three pioneer bibliographers, Andrew Maunsell,
published his remarkable *Catalogue of English Printed Books* in
1595.[6] Maunsell spoke deprecatingly of Gesner and others who mixed
up subjects in a single sequence and entered works under the authors' forenames. For his *Catalogue,* Maunsell selected a classified
subject arrangement, listing the entries within each subject alphabetically by the author's surname—a sharp departure from established custom. Other rules followed by Maunsell were entry of
anonymous works under title or subject, or both, and entry of translations under both author and translator and occasionally under
subject.

In preparing the first Harvard catalogue, Librarian Gee may
well have found the writings of the bibliographers of less use than
the published catalogues of the English and European libraries. In
the Harvard collections were the printed catalogues of two of the
most distinguished universities of the day—Leyden and Oxford. The
earliest of these catalogues, and the first printed for a general collection, was prepared for Leyden in 1595 by Petrus Bertius.[7] Published in rapid succession were Georg Henisch's catalogue of Augsburg in 1600[8] and Thomas James's catalogue of the Bodleian Library
at Oxford in 1605.[9] The Bodleian, Augsburg, and Leyden libraries
all published their second catalogue within fifty years: the Bodleian
in 1620,[10] with a supplement in 1635;[11] Augsburg in 1633;[12] and
Leyden in 1640.[13] Another catalogue of the Bodleian collections
was issued in 1674.[14]

More than the catalogues of any other library, those of the
Bodleian shaped the efforts of Gee and his American colleagues.
In fact, in the preparation of catalogues and in most other library
matters, the Bodleian exercised unchallenged leadership among
the libraries of English-speaking peoples until well after 1800.
The other great English university of the day, Cambridge, failed
to print even one catalogue of its collections during America's
colonial period. The Bodleian catalogues had the further good for-
tune of appearing in large editions which permitted their wide distribution among American libraries.

The first printed catalogue of the Bodleian Library, compiled
by Thomas James in 1605,[15] contained entries, interfiled, for about
4,000 manuscript and printed volumes. Arranged alphabetically by
author, the entries were grouped under the four academic faculties
of theology, jurisprudence, medicine, and the arts. Books of persona

authorship were entered under the author's surname; anonymous and pseudonymous works under the most significant word in the title. In addition to the author and a casual transcription of the title, the entry provided the place and date of publication, size of the volume, and its location in the library. The catalogue also made entries for all works bound together in a single physical volume. Finally, following the main catalogue was an alphabetical index of the authors' names and other entry words.

The Bodleian published its second catalogue in 1620, the year of James's resignation as librarian. Again, the entries for manuscript and printed volumes were interfiled; this time, however, rather than being grouped under the four faculties, they were listed alphabetically by entry word in a single sequence—the first time a general catalogue was so arranged. The entries varied little from those of the previous catalogue except for the introduction of cross references. This catalogue also occasioned one of the first references to the problem of printing costs. In 1621, the authorities decided that anyone using the Bodleian must purchase a copy of the catalogue to help defray the expense of printing.[16]

The last of the seventeenth-century Bodleian catalogues was a handsome folio volume of some 750 pages published in 1674. Thomas Hyde stated in the preface that nine years of exacting labor had gone into its preparation. This catalogue, like its predecessor, consisted of a single alphabetical sequence of entries. The preface contained one of the fullest statements to date of the rules followed in the preparation of the entries. When the author's surname was given, or could be ascertained, it was the entry word; anonymous works were entered under the most distinctive word in the title. Hyde's catalogue served libraries, particularly in America, as a model for many years, being widely distributed, much used, and often copied.

Although the art of catalogue making in seventeenth-century England was still in the rudimentary stages, it was more than adequate for the needs of the fledgling libraries in the Colonies. The task, rather, was to adapt this knowledge to the needs of the libraries in the new land. Predictably, the first library catalogues printed in America were simply arranged and designed for small collections; not so predictably, they were also ably edited and well printed—and for good cause. Books and money for books were sorely lacking in the Colonies; and in the catalogue the colonists astutely recognized a prime means for soliciting gifts, especially from their wealthier countrymen back in England.

LIBRARIES IN COLONIAL AMERICA

Colonial America bred libraries in profusion: college, social, town, rental or circulating, parish, and private. As a group, the college libraries were among the largest, best supported, and most permanent. Led by Harvard, each of the nine colonial colleges established a library shortly after its founding.

College Libraries

The role of the library in the colonial college is elusive. Small and poorly selected collections, cramped physical quarters, short hours of opening, restricted circulation of books, and irregular financial support would hardly suggest that colonial higher education revolved around the library. But this picture is tempered by frequent gifts of books and money, regular provision of quarters, occasional provision of financial support, and the attitude of scholars and college officers that an adequate library was the badge of academic responsibility.

Even by the standards of the day, the library collections of colonial colleges were small. Shortly before the Revolutionary War, the largest college library in America, Harvard, numbered but 5,000 volumes;[17] and its collections were considerably larger than the libraries of the other colleges. In contrast, the Bodleian Library had 16,000 volumes in 1629 and 25,000 at the end of the century; Cambridge University Library possessed 30,000 volumes at the middle of the eighteenth century.[18] When Christian Heyne became librarian in 1763, peerless Göttingen boasted 60,000 volumes; a generation later, the collection had doubled.[19]

The smallness of colonial collections has been attributed variously to the scarcity of books in the Colonies, pillage during the Revolution, and fire.[20] The investigations of Thomas G. Wright, Samuel Eliot Morison, and Louis B. Wright have largely dispelled the notion that books were difficult to come by in the Colonies.[21] As for fire and pillage, the largest collection suffering that fate was the 5,000-volume library of Harvard in 1764, the preservation of which would hardly have brought that institution abreast of her European and English sisters. A more plausible explanation is that the American libraries were simply in the stage of small beginnings.

Nor was the smallness of colonial collections offset by the excellence of their selection. Although colleges occasionally appropriated money for books, their libraries were largely the result of gifts. In fact, only about one book in ten found its way into colonial collections by direct purchase.[22] A few of the gifts were notable—

the collections which Lord Berkeley and Jeremiah Dummer gave
to Yale and which the Hollis family presented to Harvard, for example—but the majority of gifts, then as now, were books no longer
desired by their owners. Since in many instances the donors were
ministers, books on theology dominated. Many of the collections
also contained significant holdings of historical and classical
works; but in all other areas the libraries were usually deficient.

The colonial college library was available, on decreasingly
liberal terms, to the president, other governing officials, instructional officers, students pursuing advanced degrees, senior students, and junior students. Except upon rare occasion, freshmen
and sophomores were denied admittance to the library. Underlying
this regulation was the firmly embedded notion that library service
was not necessary for the proper education of undergraduate students, especially in their first years. Their education was con-
strued as being largely elementary in character, consisting of the
acquisition of certain basic facts, the understanding of a few principles, and the mastery of techniques. The undergraduate was expected to purchase the few books necessary for these purposes.

What services were available to the faculty and to those students privileged to use the library? The situation at Harvard College in 1765 was typical.[23] On every third Friday, at an appointed
hour, those students with library privileges were permitted to
borrow three books. On each Wednesday they were allowed en-
trance to the library for a short time to use books which could not
be withdrawn. For the governing and instructional officers conditions were easier. The librarian was obliged by the regulations to
open the library for them when requested. Clearly, the library in
the colonial college was not a place for the use and study of books.
Rather, it was a place for the storage and preservation of books,
and needed to be opened only a few hours each week for the lending
and returning of books.

Social Libraries

The social library, especially in the latter years of the colonial period, was the most characteristic and successful form of
"public" library. Beginning with Franklin's founding of the Library
Company of Philadelphia in 1731, at least sixty-four of these libraries appeared in the Colonies before the Revolution.[24] Among
the largest and most influential were the Library Company of Philadelphia, the Redwood Library in Newport, the Charleston Library
Society, and the New York Society Library. The social library was
usually organized on the joint-stock principle, with funds being
raised by the sale of shares of stock. Frequently, additional funds

were raised by placing an annual assessment on each share of stock.

The primary motive in founding the social library was, of course, the colonists' desire for books. By pooling their resources, they recognized that each might have access to many more books than he could hope to acquire individually. The urge for group activities and social enjoyment has also been advanced as a cause for establishing the social library.[25] Although the church had long ministered to this need, the literary club with its library provided a breadth and variety of interests which the church lacked. In the formation of the social library little importance can be assigned to the desire of the ordinary citizen to improve himself through education. Not until the nineteenth century would the myriad of young men's, apprentices', mechanics', mercantile, and, eventually, public libraries be formed to minister to this need.

The book collections of the social libraries presented a striking contrast with those of the colleges. Books on theology, dominant in the college libraries, fell increasingly from favor in the social libraries during this period. So, too, did the classics. In their places on the shelves were belles-lettres, biography, travel, history, and science. The highly traditional character of colonial higher education accounted for part of this difference, of course. Years were to pass before the natural sciences, modern languages, and history forced their way into the curriculum. The means the two types of libraries employed for building their collections also contributed. Whereas the college library was largely dependent upon gifts from its minister friends, the social library had funds to purchase directly many of the books it desired.

The first social libraries exhibited considerably more wisdom and liberality in the selection of their books than they did in their general operation. The regulations governing the borrowing and returning of books, for example, were quite restrictive. Customarily, only one or two books could be withdrawn at a time, for a period of two to four weeks. Offenders were subject to costly fines. The hours of opening were also limited—two to eight hours each week. The social libraries did, however, open their doors rather widely to nonsubscribers, who were granted borrowing privileges for a fee. Clearly, the social library, like the college library, was regarded as a storehouse for books, and only incidentally as a place for reading and study.

Although other types of libraries were present in Colonial America (some even printed an occasional catalogue), their contribution to the development of the printed book catalogue was slight.

THE FIRST AMERICAN LIBRARY CATALOGUES

Motives for Preparation

The desire to attract gifts of books bulked large in the decision of the colonial colleges to print catalogues. A catalogue was recognized to be an excellent means both for acknowledging and soliciting gifts. The immediate occasion for the printing of the first library catalogue in America was a request from Thomas Hollis, February 2, 1722, for a number of catalogues of the Harvard Library for distribution among prospective donors in England. As a result of this request, the Harvard Corporation took the following action:

> Upon the Intimation lately made by Mr Hollis, and formerly by Mr Neal, that it may be of great Advantage to the College Library, that a Catalogue of the Books in the sd Library be printed and Sent abroad, Voted, that forthwith the Library-keepr take an exact Catalogue of the Books in the Library, and that the same be printed in Order to transmitt to friends abroad: And that this be don at the Charge of the College.[26]

The idea of attracting gifts for the library was similarly in the mind of President Davies when, in the introduction to the 1760 catalogue of the College of New Jersey, he wrote:

> As some valuable Benefactions have been the sponteneous Offerings of unsolicited Charity, without any other Excitement than the Knowledge of the Poverty and public Utility of the Foundation; this Catalogue is published to give that Information to such, who are watching for Opportunities of doing Good; and to afford particular Benefactors the Pleasure of seeing how many others have concurred with them in their favourite Charity.[27]

Yale was quite as dependent upon gifts for its growth as was either Princeton or Harvard, although its 1743 catalogue did not suggest this.[28] The catalogue contained no direct appeal for gifts, and its internal arrangement suggested that it was prepared primarily to assist students in the use of the library.

The catalogues prepared for the social libraries were also promotional in character; however, instead of seeking gifts of books, they sought to enroll new members and to further their libraries generally. Appended to the earliest existing catalogue of the Library Company of Philadelphia—that of 1741—is "A Short Account of the Library" in which the advantages of membership are persuasively argued:

> As Shares encrease yearly in Value 10s. so much being
> yearly added by each Subscriber to the Stock of Books, a Share
> which at first was worth but 40s. is now valued at 6 £. 10s.
> But for this small Sum, which, laid out in Books, would go but
> a little Way, every Member has the Use of a Library now worth
> upwards of 500 £. whereby Knowledge is in this City render'd
> more cheap and easy to be come at, to the great Pleasure and
> Advantage of the studious Part of the Inhabitants. [29]

Other social libraries followed suit. In addition to listing the stock
of books, their catalogues contained short historical sketches of
the libraries, copies of the charters, lists of members, and the library rules and regulations.

In the preparation of catalogues for colonial libraries, the desire to construct an index useful to the reader was also apparent.
Even at this early date a few individuals realized the potential
value and use of a library, especially for higher education. In the
introduction to his 1760 catalogue of the College of New Jersey,
President Davies wrote:

> A large and well-sorted Collection of Books on the various
> Branches of Literature, is the most ornamental and useful
> Furniture of a College, and the most proper and valuable Fund
> with which it can be endowed. It is one of the best Helps to
> enrich the Minds both of the Officers and Students with Knowl-
> edge; to give them an extensive Acquaintance with Authors;
> and to lead them beyond the narrow Limits of the Books to
> which they are confined in their stated Studies and Recitations,
> that they may expatiate at large thro' the boundless and varie-
> gated Fields of Science. [30]

President Clap of Yale recognized that not only were well-
stocked libraries needed but also carefully prepared catalogues.
Concerning the printing of the 1743 Yale catalogue, he observed
that "before this Time there never had been any perfect Catalogue
of the Books in the Library; for want of which the Students were
deprived of much of the Benefit and Advantage of them." [31]

President Clap's forward-looking views found expression in an
occasional catalogue of the day. Two catalogues, for example, were
arranged by subject: the 1743 Yale catalogue and the 1760 Loganian. [32] Several catalogues also showed their interest in the reader
by making multiple entries for the titles. In the same 1743 classed
catalogue of the Yale Library, many books were entered under as
many as five different subjects. In the 1765 catalogue of the Philadelphia Association Library Company [33] and the 1770 catalogue of

the Library Company of Philadelphia,[34] entries frequently were
made under the first or principal word of the title as well as under
the author. It should also be noted that, in 1773, Harvard College
prepared a catalogue of selected portions of the library expressly
for the use of its undergraduate students.[35]

A final cause for the compilation of colonial catalogues was
the need for an inventory of the collections. There is little evidence, however, that the inventorial need ever led to the printing
of a catalogue. For this purpose a manuscript catalogue sufficed
equally well.

Methods of Arrangement

Once the decision to print a catalogue was reached, the plan
for arranging the entries had to be selected. The colonists had
ample precedent for the use of four different methods: subject,
alphabetization, size, and donor. In Europe throughout the Middle
Ages, the Renaissance, and until well into the seventeenth century,
the broadly classed catalogue held sway. In the seventeenth century the alphabetical author catalogue, largely as a result of its
use in the Bodleian Library, successfully challenged the older
classed or subject catalogue. The size of the books was also a
factor which was frequently introduced into the scheme of arrangement, whether classed or alphabetical; indeed, size was occasionally the only order present in the catalogue. A final method for
arranging the titles within a catalogue was by the names of the donors of books.

Of the twenty-odd library catalogues printed in Colonial America, the entries in all but three were arranged either alphabetically
or by the size of the volumes described, or by a combination of
both means. Typical were the 1723 catalogue of Harvard College,
which was arranged first by size and then alphabetically through
the first letter of the entry word; the 1760 catalogue of the College
of New Jersey which was arranged by size, after an initial subdivision by the first letter of the entry word; the 1773 catalogue of
Harvard which was completely alphabetized; and the 1741, 1757,[36]
and 1764[37] catalogues of the Library Company of Philadelphia
which had no order other than size.

A classed arrangement found its way into only three catalogues. The 1743 catalogue of Yale College was a closely classed
arrangement with each of the classes having numerous subdivisions.
There was no order within the subject groupings. The 1760 catalogue of the Loganian Library was arranged somewhat differently.
It was broadly classed, but the entries within each class were arranged by size and then alphabetically. A classed arrangement was

also used in a portion of the 1764 catalogue of the Redwood Library in Newport.[38] This catalogue, which presented a donor arrangement with a further subdivision by size, grouped the octavo-sized books given by Abraham Redwood by subject.

The contention has been made that size was the only reasonable arrangement to place before prospective donors since most private libraries were so organized.[39] This argument, while possibly accounting for the arrangement in the catalogues of college libraries, hardly explains its use in the social library catalogues, which were designed only secondarily to solicit gifts of books. The advantages which accrued from any of these various methods of arrangement were in large part lost, however, because of the undeveloped state of entries. To predict the location of a particular entry within a sequence of entries was difficult, at best.

Regardless of the method adopted for the arrangement of entries, the typical colonial catalogue provided only one entry for each title and combined all entries into a single sequence. There were, however, exceptions. The 1743 classed catalogue of Yale College entered some titles in as many as five different subject groupings. In the 1765 catalogue of the Philadelphia Association Library Company, entries were made for many books under both author and some word of the title. In its 1770 catalogue, the Library Company of Philadelphia made references to the author entry from the first or principal word of the title. The 1760 catalogue of the Loganian Library also made use of references and even included numerous entries for parts of books. Probably the only example of a colonial catalogue containing an index was the 1743 Yale catalogue. It contained at the end "An Index to the Preceding Catalogue," which was nothing more than a reproduction of the class headings used in the catalogue. Thus, although the typical catalogue was a rather simple, single-entry, single-sequence compilation, on occasion it included multiple entries, analytical entries, references, and indexes.

The pattern for the inclusion of pressmarks or some other form of book numbers in colonial catalogues is uncertain. Most of the libraries of this period used a system for numbering books that would permit their ready location. The anomaly, however, is that nearly all social libraries omitted book numbers from their catalogues, while the college libraries included them.

The systems employed for the numbering and arranging of books upon the shelves were customarily of two types. The early catalogues of Harvard and Yale carried the old pressmarks, usually in tabular form, in either the right or the left margin of the page.[40] This method, of course, fixed the physical location of every book exactly—to a particular place on a single shelf in a given "press" or bookcase. The other method, found in the 1760 Loganian catalogue and the 1765 Philadelphia Association Library Company catalogue, was to assign consecutive numbers to books, more or less in the order in which they were added to the collections. While this procedure did not fix the physical locations of books on the shelves, it allowed books to be added only at the end of the sequence. Flexible schemes that would permit the indefinite introduction of new books at any point in the sequence were to be the product of a later date.

Concept of Entry

A prerequisite for the effective use of alphabetization in arranging entries was the development of the concept of entry. The earliest catalogues obtained order among their entries by breaking them down into a few size or broad subject groupings. As long as the number of entries within each of these categories was small, any additional order among the entries was unnecessary. As the catalogues increased in size, the inconvenience of scanning several pages of entries in search of one particular entry became considerable. At this point, conditions were right for the development of the entry word, usually the first word of the entry. By this entry word the exact location of an entry within a sequence of entries could be fixed. It would be necessary, of course, to select and arrange these entry words according to a predictable scheme.

The importance of entry was appreciated by most of the colonial catalogue makers. Only five catalogues—those of Yale in 1743 and 1755 and of the Library Company of Philadelphia in 1741, 1757, and 1764—ignored the benefits to be gained from systematic entry. In the closely classed Yale catalogues, the results were not serious inasmuch as few sequences of entries exceeded a page in length. The effects in the 1764 Library Company catalogue, broken down as it was by size only, were disastrous. Consider the difficulty of finding a particular book—even granting that its size was known— among thirty pages of arbitrarily listed folio titles, sixteen pages of quarto titles, seventy-plus pages of octavo titles, or twenty-five pages of duodecimo and smaller titles!

Bibliographical Description

The rules followed in compiling entries for the colonial catalogues were modeled after those used by Thomas Hyde in his 1674 catalogue of the Bodleian Library. Hyde's rules, one of the first sizable bodies of cataloguing instructions, long served as a guide for the compilation of catalogues in the English-speaking world.

In conformity with current practice, Hyde entered books under the
surname of the author, usually in the possessive form. Occasionally, the initials or forenames of the author also were used. Then,
as now, the chief difficulties arose in making entries for works
lacking personal authors. The general practice for anonymous
works was to make entry under the principal or most distinctive
word of the title. Books of corporate authorship were so few that
the many problems they were to present to librarians of later gen-
erations went largely unnoticed. There was also little use of the
popular later practice of entering works under literary form headings, such as poetry, plays, fiction, and sermons, or under practical
form headings, such as dictionaries, catalogues, and encyclopedias.

In their preparation of the entry proper, as in their choice of
entry words, colonial catalogue makers did not stray far from the
example of their English contemporaries. That they regarded the
title page as less than sacred was evidenced by their brief and
loose title transcriptions, some of which were nothing more than
binders' titles. Imprint information, quite as often omitted as included, consisted of place and date of publication—never the publisher. The collation statement was limited to the number of volumes, and given only when the work consisted of more than one
volume. Size, if not already incorporated into the arrangement of
the catalogue, was also made a part of the entry. Notes, with a few
exceptions, were restricted to those calling attention to the donor
of the book.

The typical entry, then, was made up of the author's surname
in the possessive case, brief title, occasionally the place and date
of publication, the number and size of the volumes, and an infrequent donor note. Notable exceptions to the preceding pattern were
the entries in the catalogues of the Library Company of Philadelphia and the Loganian Library, which were full transcriptions of
the title pages.[41] In contrast to the typical entry which was a line
or two in length, these entries ran to five, six, and seven lines.

Compilers

For most of the compilers of the colonial catalogues, librarianship was a part-time occupation and catalogue making a strange
and new experience. In the earliest social libraries a member of
the group was customarily appointed custodian, without compensation. As the responsibilities of the position increased, someone
was hired to perform the duties. A similar situation existed in the
colleges where, in most instances, the first librarians were the
presidents. Soon, however, the responsibility was delegated to the
faculty—usually a junior member—where it remained in most

colleges until the nineteenth century was well under way. A member of the faculty, for example, was still assuming the library duties at Rutgers until about 1800, at Yale until 1805, at Columbia until 1837, and at the University of Pennsylvania until 1831.[42]

One result of this performance of library duties by professors as an added assignment, by part-time hired employees, and by volunteers was that special arrangements were necessary for the large task of preparing a catalogue. It was not unusual to give the person regularly performing the library duties an extra stipend for this work. At Harvard, in 1705 and again in 1709, the library keepers were allowed 40s. and 50s., respectively, for making catalogues of the collections.[43] At the University of Pennsylvania, the problem was handled more economically—a committee of three faculty members was appointed in 1774 to perform the task with no added compensation.[44] Even college presidents on occasion did not escape the duty. On the day of his inauguration as President of the College of New Jersey, Rev. Samuel Davies was requested by the Trustees to prepare a catalogue of the library. President Davies personally carried out this assignment during his first four months in office.[45] The 1743 catalogue of the Yale Library was also the result of the labors of a college president—Rector Thomas A. Clap.[46] Although the compilers of colonial catalogues were undoubtedly able men, they were not qualified for this particular duty. Too, the press of other matters did not permit them to give the task the attention it deserved.

Physical Appearance

The promotional character of colonial catalogues was evident in their handsome physical appearance. Some of the best printers in the colonies were called upon. Benjamin Franklin printed the 1733,[47] 1735,[48] 1741, 1757, 1764, and 1770 catalogues of the Library Company of Philadelphia. James Parker of Woodbridge, New Jersey, printed the 1760 Princeton catalogue, and William Bradford the 1765 catalogue of the Association Library Company of Philadelphia. The catalogues were small in format and seldom ran to more than one hundred pages in length. The type was set up in a single column with generous margins on either edge of the page. In most instances a line of text accommodated the entry for a single title. Italicized type was frequently used to set off the entry words, class headings, or places of publication. Clearly, the day of the large, unattractive catalogue with its small type and crowded pages had not yet arrived.

Size, Cost, and Frequency of Editions

Although only scattered information is available, there can be no doubt that colonial catalogues were printed in small and infrequent editions. The 1723 catalogue of Harvard College, for example, appeared in only 300 copies;[49] the 1773 catalogue of the New York Society Library in only 500 copies.[50] The editions of the catalogues of the Library Company of Philadelphia were no larger. Their 1741 catalogue appeared in 200 copies, the 1764 catalogue in 400 copies, and the 1770 catalogue in 600 copies.[51] The majority of the copies of the college library catalogues were distributed among prospective donors; the catalogues of the society libraries, of course, went primarily to members.

It is regrettable that fuller information is not available on the costs of preparing and printing colonial catalogues. For the 1723 catalogue of Harvard College, however, we do have some information.[52] The librarian, Joshua Gee, contracted with a printer, Bartholomew Green, to have the catalogue issued in an edition of 300 copies at 30s. per sheet. Considering that the catalogue was octavo in format and had 106 pages, the total cost should have been a little over £20. As the work progressed, Green discovered that his original quotation was far too low and applied to the Corporation for relief. The final cost of printing was, apparently, around £35. For his efforts in supplying copy, Gee was allowed £20 which brought the total cost of the catalogue to about £55—not, it would seem, an unreasonable figure. In the absence of other discussions on the difficulties of financing catalogues, and in view of the small collections and simplicity of cataloguing procedures, bringing a catalogue to press was obviously not the arduous task it later became.

In this discussion of colonial library catalogues, the impression should not be left that the usual practice of libraries was to print catalogues of their collections. Indeed, quite the opposite was true, for the great majority of the libraries printed no catalogues during this period. Eighty-five years passed before Harvard College published its first catalogue. Of the other eight colonial colleges, only Yale and Princeton published catalogues. The social libraries did little better. Of the sixty-four such libraries which Thompson says were founded before the Revolution, only five are known to have prepared and printed catalogues.[53] In the absence of printed catalogues, however, it should not be concluded that colonial libraries had no lists of their collections. The literature concerning early libraries is replete with references to the compilation of manuscript catalogues. But pertinent to this discussion is which libraries printed catalogues, and how often.

A direct relationship existed between the size and affluence of libraries and the printing of catalogues. Among the social libraries the Library Company of Philadelphia, the Redwood Library of Newport, the Charleston Library Society, and the New York Society Library constituted the elite. All four published catalogues. The Library Company of Philadelphia published catalogues in 1733, 1735, 1741, 1757, 1764, and 1770; no copies of the 1733 and 1735 catalogues survived. The New York Society Library, founded in 1754, published catalogues in 1758,[54] 1761,[55] and 1773. The Charleston Library Society did not publish its first catalogue until 1770,[56] some twenty years after its founding. Almost as long a period after its founding elapsed before the Redwood Library of Newport issued its first printed catalogue in 1764.

A similar situation existed among the libraries of the colonial colleges. Pre-eminent among these institutions were, of course, Harvard, Yale, William and Mary, and the College of New Jersey, later Princeton. Of these, all but William and Mary published catalogues. Harvard published its first catalogue in 1723, with supplements in 1725 and 1735. A catalogue of selected portions of the library appeared in 1773. Yale printed its first catalogue in 1743 and reprinted it with slight additions in 1755. Princeton published its only colonial catalogue in 1760. The other colonial colleges—Columbia, Pennsylvania, Brown, Rutgers, and Dartmouth—published no catalogues during this period.

Chapter II

Beginnings of Modern Catalogues, 1780-1850

During the first half of the nineteenth century, one consideration
progressively dominated the preparation of catalogues—the need
for an index to assist the reader in his use of the library. This
resulted, although indirectly of course, from a number of changes
in American life, all of which pointed up the individual's need for
more education. His ability to participate in the new democracy,
to keep pace in a rapidly industrializing society, and to fulfill other
roles thrust upon him by nineteenth-century American life suddenly
depended largely upon his education. To help provide this education he joined his fellow men to establish libraries in unprecedented
numbers. Apprentices', mechanics', mercantile, society, historical, and governmental libraries sprang up throughout the land; even
the college libraries stirred. In the formation of these libraries,
the primary intention was not to preserve the books for future gen-
erations; rather, it was to organize them for immediate use. As
both librarians and readers were to discover shortly, this was not
a simple task.

Few of the aids which modern librarianship furnishes readers
were present in the early nineteenth century. Largely lacking, for
example, were the printed bibliographies, periodical indexes,
reading guides, and other reference books considered so necessary
today. Nor were the library attendants of much help to readers.
Tradition as yet limited the librarian's role to procuring and
checking out books; not until much later would the giving of reference assistance to readers be a part of his duties. Lastly, the
reader was denied the opportunity to help himself, for he was for-
bidden to browse among the shelves and to select the books he
wished.

Under these conditions readers quickly came to regard the

16

catalogue as the "key" to the library. As such, many improvements were necessary in its make-up. The catalogue was expected to provide an approach not only to the individual volumes of the collection but also to their subject content. To accomplish this, new methods of arrangement were introduced and improvements in technique adopted. Although by 1850 the catalogue was not the finished tool it eventually became, it had firmly established itself as an indispensable part of the modern library. To possess such a catalogue, up-to-date and in printed form, was the goal, although often unrealized, of every library in the country.

LIBRARIES IN A NEW SOCIETY

College Libraries

The middle of the nineteenth century found higher education in America little changed from the colonial period. Events of the intervening years, however, had rendered the traditional liberal arts curriculum, with its emphasis upon the classical languages, increasingly unsatisfactory. Indeed, many of the forces that would eventually alter higher education were already in evidence.

Foremost among these was the long-standing dissatisfaction with the narrowness of the curriculum and its hostility toward new fields of study. Among the earliest and most significant protests were those voiced by Jefferson and Franklin.[1] Although both men were confident of the value of the classics, Jefferson wished to supplement the traditional curriculum with newer subjects such as history, government, science, and modern languages, while Franklin sought to set up a parallel course more suited to the needs of those young men who would follow the "mechanic profession." In the following years other men voiced their dissatisfaction, but with little success. Although occasional instruction in history, the natural sciences, and modern languages was given in 1850, the traditional curriculum remained substantially intact. The task of gaining entry and acceptance for the newer disciplines was to await President Eliot of Harvard and the introduction of the system of free election of courses.

In addition to broadening education, there was also sentiment for extending it upward—for graduate study. The example of the German university was well known in America, and the great migration of American students to Germany, which was to number ten thousand before the outbreak of the First World War, had already begun.[2] But, once more, conditions were such that some twenty-five years would elapse before America's first graduate school opened its doors. At the middle of the nineteenth century few people in America viewed research and graduate study as proper concerns of higher education.

Considerable dissatisfaction was also expressed with the entrenched textbook-recitation method of instruction. This system, many argued, was more appropriate for secondary school students. The lecture method, at the time being used effectively in German universities, succeeded in making some headway, notably in the teaching of the natural sciences. But, again, the *status quo* was not to be disturbed. Attitudes toward the library and its use would change little until the textbook fell from favor and the lecture and German research methods were introduced. As late as 1828 the Yale faculty warmly endorsed and reaffirmed their faith in the textbook-recitation form of instruction.[3]

Note should also be made in this cursory survey that in 1850 the agricultural and technical schools were not yet born. Prior to the passage of the Morrill Act in 1862, only six institutions of higher education purported to concern themselves with such matters.[4] Although a few states had established universities before 1850, the American state university, as a distinct type of educational institution, was yet to evolve.

Such was the American college in 1850—much as it had been two hundred years before except that it was ready for change. It would have been unusual, indeed, had a similar situation not existed in the libraries serving higher education. James H. Canfield, writing in 1902, summarized their plight thus:

> Fifty years ago the college library was almost an aside in education. Indeed, it was much like the sentence which we inclose in brackets: to be read in a low tone, or to be slurred over hastily, or even to be entirely omitted without making any serious change in the sense.... The appropriations for maintenance were pitifully meager. The expenditures for expansion were even less worthy. The efficiency, or inefficiency, was, naturally, quite proportionate....[5]

There is little to suggest that Canfield overstated his case.

Collections were still pitifully small, especially when compared to college and university libraries abroad. Jewett in 1850 found only one American college library with more than 25,000 volumes—Harvard, with about 75,000.[6] At this time Göttingen was credited with 360,000 volumes, the Bodleian with 220,000, Tübingen and Munich with 200,000, and Cambridge with 166,724.[7] Nor were American libraries closing the gap. During the decade of the 1840's, Harvard was adding annually only about 2,040 volumes; Brown, 1,400; Yale, 950; Virginia, 410; and Columbia, 120.[8]

Hard-pressed even to keep their doors open, colleges seldom

were able to appropriate funds for their libraries. A few of the
more fortunate libraries possessed small endowments for books
which yielded from $100 to $200 annually. Other institutions periodically conducted fund-raising drives to secure money for the
purchase of books. Most unusual was the Brown University Library which raised $20,000 in eight years.[9]

Even with the benefit of one hundred years' perspective, few
present-day historians would care to take issue with Jewett's judgment of American collections in 1850:

> Our colleges are mostly eleemosynary institutions. Their
> libraries are frequently the chance aggregations of the gifts of
> charity; too many of them discarded, as well nigh worthless,
> from the shelves of the donors. This is not true of all our
> college libraries; for among them are a few of the choicest
> and most valuable collections in the country....[10]

Among these choice collections was Jewett's own library, Brown.
Harvard, of course, even then was a mecca for scholars throughout the country. Other outstanding collections were the small but
well-selected libraries of the University of Virginia and of the
Andover Theological Seminary.

During this period genuine progress was made in extending
library hours. Although many of the libraries were still open only
a few hours a week, Yale was open thirty hours a week, Brown and
South Carolina twenty-four. And the libraries which still denied
service to their lower-level students were becoming increasingly
rare. Among the larger schools only Yale and Columbia lagged.[11]

College students of this era are to be commended in that they
did not passively accept the meager course offerings and the inadequate libraries. In dissatisfaction and in protest there arose on
most of the campuses an institution known as the "student society,"
which was designed "to exercise and improve its members in ora-
tory, composition, and forensic discussion."[12] To carry on their
programs these societies customarily established their own libraries. Of the colleges in existence in 1830, fully 80 per cent had society libraries, half of which were larger than the college libraries.[13] Since the collections in the student libraries were well selected and freely available they were frequently the only libraries
used by the students. Although some of the collections were quite
broad in scope, the emphasis was upon the current literature of the
day, including the leading journals of opinion. In 1850, Jewett noted
that "dust seldom gathers on the books in such collections."[14] In
many respects the student libraries were the real college libraries
of the day.

Other "Public" Libraries

There was no lack of other "public" libraries in the United
States during the first half of the nineteenth century. It is doubtful
whether another age in history has witnessed the founding of such
a multitude of libraries by such a variety of groups. Before the
end of the period almost every hamlet had its library, and not infrequently two or three. Dominating the scene was the social library and its numerous subspecies: the young men's library, the
mercantile library, the mechanics' library, and the apprentices'
library.

The conditions which gave rise to the society library were
numerous and complex. During the colonial period, it may be recalled, the society library was not an especially democratic institution, its benefits seldom extending below the upper strata of the
population. As the young democracy matured, however, it became
apparent that basic to this form of government was an educated and
informed citizenry. All members of the society must possess an
equal educational opportunity, and that opportunity must be substantial.

Occurring at the same time was the industrialization of America. Society became intense, specialized, and highly competitive.
The individual, if he was not to be left behind, had constantly to
improve himself. Accompanying the industrialization of American
society were certain social evils. To combat these evils and to
save American youth were the primary concerns of the great hu-
manitarian movement which swept through the nation. These, in
brief, were the stimuli for the formation of the society libraries—
with all of their variations—and were the same stimuli which eventually produced the American public library.

The objectives of the society libraries, unlike those of the college libraries, were specific, real, and vigorously pursued. Their
collections, although small, were carefully chosen and—in sharp
contrast to those of the colleges—used. The New York Mercantile
Library reported in 1850, for example, a circulation of 75,000
books among their 1,000 members; the same year the Boston Mercantile Library announced that their 1,100 members had withdrawn
28,000 books.[15] Whereas the college libraries were open but a few
hours each week, the society libraries were open several hours
each day. In 1850, the New York Mercantile Library was open from
ten o'clock in the morning until ten in the evening; the Cincinnati
Young Men's Mercantile Library opened an hour earlier and closed
at ten in the evening; the Hartford Young Men's Institute Library
opened daily at ten o'clock and closed at nine in the evening; and
the Buffalo Young Men's library was open daily from eight in the

morning until nine in the evening.[16] Membership rates in the society libraries were reasonable and probably discouraged few readers. The annual $2 fees assessed by the Boston and the New York Mercantile libraries were typical, other than for a few of the older, more exclusive associations.[17]

Had the society libraries been able to maintain the excellent performances described above—performances not unusual for most of them in their earlier years—the free public library might never have been born. Unfortunately, however, they seldom were able to retain the enthusiasm of their founders, and they failed to solve the recurrent weakness of all voluntary organizations—irregular and insufficient financial support. As a consequence, with disheartening regularity the story of the society libraries was "growth, decline, and neglect."[18] Clearly, this was not a satisfactory base upon which to build library service.

The growth and development of American society were also reflected in government, both at the national and at the state levels. Various governmental units found it necessary to organize libraries of their own in order to carry out their expanding duties. By 1850, the Library of Congress, several other units of the national government, and forty of the states had formally organized their libraries, several of which rapidly became distinguished.[19]

Also contributing to the proliferation of libraries was an increased interest in scholarship, particularly historical. American students who had studied in the great research libraries abroad were acutely conscious of the scarcity of books in America and were not averse to so stating. Typical of their comments was the often quoted remark of the Anglophile Fisher Ames that the combined resources of all American libraries could not have produced a single work such as Gibbon's [20] *Decline and Fall of the Roman Empire*. For the young American scholar this was cause both for national embarrassment and for action. As a result, many of the great American historical and learned society libraries were formed in these years.

PUBLIC CATALOGUE—"KEY TO THE LIBRARY"

Motives for Preparation

In an era in which readers received little assistance from librarians and even less from bibliographies and indexes, the catalogue quite properly was regarded as an invaluable tool. Indeed, the statement of James Cox in the preface to the 1840 *Catalogue* of the Philadelphia Mercantile Library suggested an almost complete dependence upon the catalogue: "The members...will require no other assistance than this catalogue to find such books as they may desire."[21] This sentiment was repeated, with lengthy embellishment, by Edward Johnston in the introduction to the 1837 *Systematic Catalogue* ... of the New York Mercantile Library Association:

> ... The student may, with no assistance but his catalogue, find, in a body, all that is proper to each matter of learning, and whatever the collection contains to elucidate it. An aid of this kind is indispensable to the usefulness of every collection the instant it reaches a size permitting it to be useful at all. Without this, even he who is most versed in books is forced laboriously to search out and collect, from the mere chaos of volumes, those which relate to the immediate object of his inquiries; while he whose knowledge is yet to form wanders through a labyrinth without a clew. The directors, in a word, were led to consider that a library is useful just in proportion as it possesses a guide to its contents; an index, that, to the savant, saves his time and pains; and to the young adventurer in knowledge, going to sea for the first time, supplies a compass and a chart. [22]

Whereas the desire to make the book collection useful was the primary reason for compiling catalogues, the promotional idea, so prominent in the colonial era, was still much in evidence. The situation could hardly have been otherwise, dependent as libraries were upon gifts for their growth. Illustrative of the thinking that the catalogue was an admirable means for soliciting gifts was the statement which Rev. Timothy Alden, President of Allegheny College, included in the 1823 library catalogue of that institution:

> The object in publishing this Catalogue is, not only, to manifest the respectful gratitude of the Trustees, the Faculty of Arts, the Students, and the Friends of this western Seminary, for the, in United States, unprecedented patronage, which one department in this new institution has had; but that its friends, at home and abroad, seeing what has already been bestowed, may perceive what is wanted to increase its literary and scientific treasures, and with the well founded hope and expectation that not a few, who delight in using their endeavours to diffuse the light of knowledge in a new flourishing, and interesting section of the American republic, will, from time to time, gratify their inclination and enhance the obligations, which are sincerely felt, by adding, as opportunity may offer, to the Library of Alleghany [sic] College, publications on any art or science and in any language whatever.[23]

Financial Problems

If the value of the printed catalogue was widely appreciated during the first half of the nineteenth century, so also was the cost of bringing it to press. The reason was readily apparent. In a period in which libraries were continually beset by inadequate funds, the expense of printing a catalogue constituted an especial hardship. The cost of printing 500 copies of a catalogue of from 300 to 400 pages amounted to approximately $500.[24] In all but the largest libraries, this sum was more than was ordinarily expended for books in an entire year. The libraries hastened to assure themselves, however, that the catalogues were well worth the price and that the larger share of the cost would be recovered through the sale of the catalogues. Such was all too frequently not the case, as was learned by the New York Mercantile Library Association shortly after it published its 1830 catalogue: "It will be observed that the charge [$412.60] for printing catalogues, has contracted our means for the purchase of books very materially, while the number sold, has contributed but little to the funds."[25]

Although many libraries did not have funds to print catalogues as frequently as they might have desired, there were few libraries—finances permitting—who would have questioned the wisdom or the economy of the printed catalogue. The great rival and eventual successor of the printed book catalogue—the card catalogue—was still viewed primarily as a means of providing up-to-date copy for the next printed catalogue and as a tool for the librarians' use. Some ten years were to elapse before Ezra Abbot would announce that Harvard's card catalogues were "freely and conveniently accessible to all who use the Library."[26]

What might be in store for American libraries as they labored to keep up-to-date printed lists of their expanding collections was early recognized by at least one individual. Joseph Green Cogswell, an American scholar and librarian who had studied widely in Europe, noted that in 1849 only two of the forty-eight largest libraries in England and on the Continent possessed printed catalogues current to within the last ten years.[27] This was far from the situation in the United States at that time. Of the forty largest libraries, one third had printed lists of their holdings within the previous five years, and one half within the previous ten years.[28]

Arrangement

Difficult as was the financing of the printed catalogue, in the minds of many librarians its actual preparation was even more arduous. The librarian of the American Antiquarian Society, when asked to consider printing a new catalogue in 1850, declared that "there are no problems in art or science that have been found more perplexing in practice, or more incapable of a satisfactory theoretical solution.... Men have become insane," he continued, "in their efforts to reduce these labors to a system; and several instances are recorded where life has been sacrificed in consequence of the mental and physical exertion required for the completion of a catalogue in accordance with the author's view of the proper method of executing such a task."[29] What problems involved in the preparation of catalogues could have caused men to so despair, and, we might add, to be so challenged?

Not the least of these was the search for the best method of arranging the entries within the catalogue. Although this matter had long concerned catalogue makers, it assumed added importance once the catalogue was expected to be an index of the collection. To devise a catalogue that would accomplish this purpose required the best efforts of many men for many years.

In colonial America, it will be recalled, library catalogues were customarily arranged alphabetically by author. Efforts to arrange the entries in other and perhaps more useful ways were hindered by the custom of listing each title but once—a practice inherited from an earlier era in which catalogues were primarily inventories. Although the simple alphabetical arrangement permitted a book to be readily found if its author was known, it provided no subject approach whatsoever to the books in the collection.

The desire for the catalogue to serve as an index gradually led to the reintroduction of an arrangement widely used centuries before—a grouping of entries under broad subjects. This subject arrangement, its proponents argued, enabled the reader to see what books the collection possessed on a given topic; at the same time, a particular book in the collection could still be located simply by looking under the appropriate subject grouping, where the books were arranged alphabetically by author. For the critical task of dividing the collection into subject divisions, Francis Bacon's renowned classification of knowledge—with many variations—was customarily employed. Although the arrangement of catalogues was a matter concerning which agreement could not easily be obtained, the early nineteenth-century practice clearly favored the arrangement by broad subject groupings. Indeed, the larger libraries employed this method almost exclusively in the catalogues they published prior to 1820.[30]

Those libraries that published alphabetical catalogues frequently did so only with misgivings and after apologies. The 1793 alphabetical catalogue of the New York Society Library was prefaced with this explanation:

It was intended to class the books under distinct heads, so
as to have presented nearly at one view, all those that relate
to any particular subject, art, or science: But as that will be
a work of labour, not to be accomplished without time and
pains, and as there was not any complete printed Catalogue, it
was judged expedient to prepare the present one. . . . A more
systematical arrangement is therefore postponed until the
Library is increased by new acquisitions, and opportunity
offers to execute the same, in a manner more useful to readers of every description. [31]

Similar explanations were advanced in defense of the alphabetical
catalogues published by Allegheny College in 1823[32] and by the
Boston Athenaeum in 1827.[33]

A few libraries attempted to obtain the benefits of both the
broadly classed catalogue and the alphabetical catalogue by adopting a modification of the alphabetico-classed arrangement. In the
1790 catalogue of Harvard University, the entries were arranged
alphabetically under some sixty broad subjects or classes which,
in turn, were arranged alphabetically.[34] The same arrangement
was employed in the 1809 catalogue of the Baltimore Library
Company.[35] In neither catalogue, however, were the classes sub-
divided. As a result, the arrangement had little to recommend it
over the broadly classed catalogue and, consequently, was infrequently used.

Toward the end of the first quarter of the nineteenth century,
librarians were beginning to reflect upon and to state rather con-
cisely what they expected of their catalogues. In 1824, a Committee charged with the preparation of a catalogue for the library of
the American Philosophical Society phrased their thoughts thus:

[The Committee] have had two objects principally in view,
the one that the members might be able to find the books that
they should want with the greatest possible ease, the other that
those students who may wish to avail themselves of our collection, might see at one glance all that we possess relating to
the subjects of their particular researches.[36]

Two years later a similar Committee of the Charleston Library
Society stated the matter even more succinctly, adding a third re-
quirement which admittedly was of less importance:

The objects for which Catalogues of books are consulted
may be reduced to three.

1.   To ascertain whether any given book is to be found in the Library to which the Catalogue belongs.

2. To learn what books on any specified subjects are contained in
    the Library.
3. To discover what editions of particular books, what specimens
    of early typography, what works from celebrated presses, are
    in the possession of the Library.[37]

With this clearer understanding of the purposes of the catalogue
came a growing awareness of the limitations inherent in any catalogue constructed on the basis of a single entry per line. Whether
the entries were arranged alphabetically in a single sequence or
alphabetically under several broad subjects mattered little. The
former arrangement enabled the reader to find a particular book
readily but furnished him no subject approach; the latter arrangement provided the subject approach but permitted the reader to
find a particular book only if he correctly guessed under which
class it was listed.

In their efforts to find a catalogue that would perform both
functions, the librarians of the day were forced to make a basic
departure from traditional cataloguing practice. They abandoned
the idea that the catalogue should consist of but one entry for each
title and of but one sequence of entries. Their solution, logically
enough, was to retain the currently popular arrangement by broad
subjects and to add an alphabetical index of authors, sometimes
broadened to include editors, translators, and anonymous titles.

One of the first libraries to use this arrangement was the Library Company of Philadelphia in their 1789 catalogue.[38] This plan
was not employed again until 1815 when the Library of Congress
published a similar catalogue.[39] A decade later several libraries
followed suit: the American Philosophical Society in 1824, the
Charleston Library Society in 1826, and countless other libraries
in the years that followed.[40]

Although the above method of arrangement was widely and
successfully used during the second quarter of the nineteenth century, it was not employed in the outstanding catalogues of that day
and did not reflect the thinking of the leading librarians. This distinction was reserved for an arrangement which might be described
as its reverse, i.e., one in which an alphabetical listing of the entries comprised the main sequence, with a classified index of subjects added. One of the first catalogues in America to be arranged
thus was that prepared by George Campbell in 1807 for the Philadelphia Library Company.[41]

The main part of the catalogue was a full listing, alphabetically
by author, of all except anonymous works. To this list was appended
an "Index to the names of Authors and Editors ... classed under
distinct Heads," and it was precisely that. The surnames of the
authors and editors were arranged alphabetically under some thirty

broad subjects which were, in turn, arranged alphabetically. The anonymous works were listed but a single time—in a classed sequence. At the time it was printed, Campbell's catalogue caused little excitement among librarians; some twenty years later, however, the appearance of another catalogue prepared along similar lines was widely acclaimed and established a new trend in the arrangement of catalogues.

The catalogue referred to is the three-volume work prepared by Benjamin Peirce in 1830 for the library of Harvard University.[42] The first two volumes were devoted to an alphabetical listing of some 30,000 volumes in the Harvard collections, with considerable attention being given to the selection of entries and to the use of cross references. A "Systematic Index" to Volumes I and II made up the first part of the third volume, and a listing of maps and charts comprised the second part. Peirce's "Systematic Index" was one of the first uses in America of the famous book classification employed by Jacques Charles Brunet in his *Manuel du libraire et de l'amateur de livres*. [43] To Brunet's five classes, Peirce added a sixth, "Works Relating to America." All of the classes had numerous subdivisions. Within each sequence the entries were arranged alphabetically and keyed to the main alphabetical sequence through the use of the same entry words.

How deliberately Peirce selected his form of arrangement is a matter for speculation. His own words suggest that he would have preferred the main sequence of entries to have been grouped by broad subject:

> The circumstances, under which the printing of the Catalogue was commenced, seemed to require that it should be an alphabetical one; but during the progress of the work a strong desire was felt to provide some expedient which should make it answer the purpose of a classed catalogue; and it was thought that this might be done by means of a systematic index. [44]

Nevertheless, Peirce's catalogue must be accepted as he presented it, and his methods would be adopted shortly by two of the ablest bibliographers of the day: Oliver A. Taylor and his student, Charles Coffin Jewett.

Unlike Peirce, Rev. Oliver A. Taylor labored under no confusion when he embarked on the preparation of the 1838 catalogue of the Andover Theological Seminary.[45] His announced objective was nothing less than "to exhibit a full and perfect alphabetical description of everything the library contains."[46] To this alphabetical listing, which Taylor considered to be the proper foundation for any library catalogue, he planned to append a systematic index.

Unfortunately this index never appeared. Taylor's alphabetical
catalogue, however, was described by Jewett as having "no superior among printed catalogues of libraries."[47] Certainly in America no previously published catalogue exhibited comparable method
and skill in the discovery and listing of the names of authors, in
the use of added entries and cross references, and in the accuracy
and completeness of the bibliographical descriptions. Taylor also
included in the catalogue brief biographical notices for many of the
authors and bibliographical comments on many of the books. Taylor seems not to have been unaware of the excellence of his work,
for he warned his readers:

> Every error deserving the name, so far as any have been dis-
> covered, is noticed at the close of the volume. Let the reader
> at least be careful how he fancies he finds others.[48]

Even if Taylor had not compiled the excellent Andover catalogue, the library profession would still be much in his debt, for it
was he who introduced Charles Coffin Jewett to library work. During Jewett's student days at Andover, he attracted the attention of
Taylor, who asked him to assist in the preparation of the 1838 catalogue.[49] When Jewett brought out his notable catalogue of Brown
University in 1843, he freely acknowledged his great debt to Taylor:

> ...I have followed the plan of Mr. O. A. Taylor's Cata-
> logue of the Library of the Theological Seminary in Andover,
> Mass.; a work far superior to all others of the kind, which
> have been published in this country, and which has been pro-
> nounced in Germany a model for a Catalogue.[50]

Jewett was giving no more than due credit, for his catalogue was
remarkably similar to the Andover catalogue. Jewett, like Taylor,
made entry under the author when it could be determined, and when
it could not, under the most important word of the title, with full
cross references. Included, also, were biographical notes and
bibliographical comments on many of the works. Unlike Taylor,
Jewett made frequent use of such headings as "Great Britain" and
"United States," gathering under them anonymous works, sometimes but indirectly related. He also made use of form headings
such as "Catalogues," "Encyclopaedias," and "Poetry."

To the full alphabetical author listing described above, Jewett
appended a remarkable index of subjects. Although he had little
enthusiasm for the usual subject indexes, arranged according to
one of the various book classification schemes, Jewett was much
attracted to the method of arrangement lately used in the catalogue
of the Signet Library in Edinburgh. He explained his variation of

it thus: "The Index of Subjects, I have endeavored to arrange in
such a manner as to answer the purpose of an alphabetical index,
and as far as possible of a classed index."[51] Jewett sought to accomplish this by arranging in a single alphabetical sequence: (1)
entries under that word of the title judged most important, i.e.,
subject-word entries;[52] (2) entries under broad subjects; and (3)
entries under specific subjects.

Examples of all three types of entries are found on the very
first page of the Index. Such entries as "Affections, Religious,"
"Alexandrian Aqueduct," and "Allegiance, General Claim to" illustrate the first type; "Agriculture" and "America" the second; and,
"Acoustics," "Air," and "Algebra" the third. Of especial significance was Jewett's use of the specific subject entries. In some
instances these entries were true subject entries—not subject-
word entries—in that the word selected as the subject did not appear in the titles listed under it. The way was now open for the
compilation of a full dictionary catalogue.

Jewett's catalogue was reviewed widely and enthusiastically in
the periodical press of the day, with his views on the arrangement
of catalogues being particularly well received. Jewett undoubtedly
received special satisfaction when he read the following comment
in the *North American Review:*

> We think, therefore, that Mr. Jewett has done wisely in
> adopting the alphabetical arrangement both for the descriptive
> catalogue and the index of subjects. It is true, that the order
> of the alphabet does not seem a very scientific one; but in this
> instance, as in many others, it happens, that the system which
> has the least appearance of science is the most convenient for
> use.[53]

The alphabetical catalogue appeared with still another arrangement of the subject index—the alphabetico-classed. The New York
Mercantile Library in its 1844 catalogue rejected the classed arrangement in its subject index in favor of an alphabetico-classed
because they judged that "what is lost ... as respects the appearance of scientific accuracy is more than supplied on the plan
adopted in our Catalogue, by the greater practical convenience it
affords."[54] The entries, brief author-title transcriptions, were
alphabetically arranged under sixty-nine subjects which were, in
turn, arranged alphabetically. In the succeeding years few libraries followed the example of the New York Mercantile Library.

Whether a catalogue appeared during this period which could
properly be described as "dictionary" in its arrangement is ques-
tionable. The answer is no, of course, if the strict definition of a
dictionary catalogue is retained, i.e., one in which entries for

authors, titles, subjects, and forms of literature are all interfiled
in a single alphabetical sequence. The position might be taken,
however, that the crucial step in the development of the dictionary
catalogue occurred when entries were first interfiled in the same
sequence which traditionally had been filed in separate sequences
within the catalogue. This occurred in the 1844 catalogue of the
Boston Mercantile Library, with the systematic entry of all works
under both author and title and with the interfiling of these entries
in a single alphabetical sequence. Since the title entries were
under the most important word of the title, they approximated subject entries in many instances. Perhaps because of this Maysel O.
Baker has described the 1844 Boston Mercantile Library catalogue
as one of the first dictionary catalogues in America.[55]

It could be argued with equal logic that only with the appearance of specific subject entries was the full dictionary arrangement
possible. Of the other means for achieving a subject approach, the
classed method lent itself not at all to the dictionary arrangement,
and the alphabetico-classed only slightly. Under this argument,
the interfiling of author and title entries could be viewed as a not
very momentous event since for years title entries had been added
to author entries to increase the usefulness of catalogues.

In selecting the method of arrangement to be used in catalogues, the manner in which the books were arranged on the shelves
of the library was seldom a consideration. At this time books usually were given fixed locations; but, even so, they were arranged
by a number of different criteria: size, broad subject, order of
acquisition, alphabet, and by combinations of the foregoing.[56] No
relationship existed, apparently, between the arrangement selected
for listing the books in the catalogue and the order chosen for placing the volumes on the shelves.

Determination of Entries

Librarians of the nineteenth century, in their efforts to prepare useful catalogues, soon discovered that the arrangement of
the entries was no more crucial than the selection of the entry
words, i.e., those words according to which the entries were filed.
Whether the entries were arranged alphabetically in one long sequence or alphabetically under several broad subjects was of slight
assistance to the reader unless he knew the entry word for the
particular book he was seeking. It was thus of utmost importance
that the entry words be determined logically, systematically, and
in a manner predictable by the reader.

Early in the nineteenth century, while collections in America
were still small and the index function of the catalogue not fully

recognized, rather casual methods of entry served reasonably well. Works were entered under the surname of the author, or, if the author was unknown, under either the first or the most important word of the title. As collections grew, the need for establishing entries systematically became more apparent. Statements of practice began to appear in the prefaces of catalogues and to be discernible from the entries themselves. Although no extended set of rules appeared in America during this period, a cataloguing code which markedly influenced American practices was published in 1841 in England—the famous ninety-one rules drafted by Anthony Panizzi for the projected British Museum catalogue.[57]

British Museum rules were characterized by a high regard for the wording of the title page. Entry was made under the author only when his name appeared somewhere in the work. Thus, anonymous and pseudonymous publications, even though their real author was known, remained anonymous and pseudonymous. Works lacking a personal author were listed under title only when several other procedures failed to produce an entry. Preferred was the entry under a person about whom the work dealt, providing that his name appeared in the title. Next choice was entry under an organization or place mentioned in the title. If the title proper furnished no entry, an editor or translator was selected.

Only when all of the foregoing procedures had been unsuccessful was entry finally made under the first substantive word of the title. Corporate, or "organization" entries as they were commonly termed, were made under the name of the place in which the organization was located or under the name of the area with which it was concerned. Exceptions were the publications of academies, universities, and other learned societies which were all arranged by place under the term, "Academies." Various form headings were adopted for special classes of materials: "Periodical Publications" for newspapers, magazines, and annuals; "Ephemerides" for almanacs and calendars; "Liturgies" for liturgies, prayer books, missals, and the like.

The differences between Panizzi's ninety-one rules and the brief and usually unstated rules used in the preparation of the better American catalogues were differences in articulation and in fullness, not in basic views regarding entry. Central to the entry concepts of both was the idea of personal authorship, with rules being phrased in the context of publications either having or not having personal authors.

Since the difficulties involved in determining entries for works with personal authors were comparatively slight, both Panizzi and his American contemporaries employed the personal author entry whenever they felt its use was defensible. The Americans, however, gave evidence of being willing to expand the idea of personal authorship beyond Panizzi's definition. In the 1823 catalogue of Allegheny College, Alden stated that anonymous works would be listed under their authors, if known, even though their names did not appear in the books.[58] This policy was adopted both by Taylor in the 1838 Andover catalogue and by Jewett in the 1843 Brown catalogue.

Although both Panizzi and his American colleagues found works without personal authors considerably more complex, they attacked them similarly. For entry words both sought to extract proper nouns from the title. In proper nouns both a rough approximation of the subject of the work and a certain precision of statement were obtained. When appropriate proper nouns were lacking in the title, practices varied. Panizzi, it will be recalled, then made entry under the first substantive in the title, while American practice tended to enter under the leading word of the title. Neither saw any essential unity in the title as it appeared on the title page and, accordingly, failed to adopt the later practice of entering anonymous works under the first word of the title.

By the middle of the nineteenth century corporate authorship existed in fact, if not in theory. Although Panizzi regarded corporate publications as but a part of the great body of anonymous works, he did recognize them as a particular type and devised special rules for their treatment.[59] These rules constitute, of course, the foundation for our present rules for corporate entry. American practices regarding corporate publications seldom progressed to the point of formulating specific rules for their entry. An exception was the 1824 catalogue of the American Philosophical Society in which the compiler stated that "the memoirs and transactions of learned societies, are classed in the order of the names of the places where those institutions are established, as London, Paris, Philadelphia, alphabetically."[60]

American librarians of the period could not, of course, escape contending with the problems of corporate publications. Their entries, characterized by an almost complete lack of consistency, appear to have resulted from efforts to select the leading word of the title. In the otherwise excellent 1830 catalogue of the Harvard Library, society publications are entered variously under the place of the society, some word in the name of the society, and the first or leading word of the title. If catalogues were to serve as finding lists, more effective methods of handling corporate publications obviously would have to be found.

With the development of the catalogue as a finding list came a more liberal and intelligent use of cross references. Panizzi devoted fifteen of his ninety-one rules to the proper construction of cross references.[61] No similar codification appeared for the

practices of an American library; in fact, even such statements as
that of Peirce that the 1830 Harvard catalogue was equipped "with
such references ... as it was thought would be found useful" were
rare.[62] In the absence of more specific rules the use of cross references in American catalogues was understandably haphazard.

As the procedures for establishing entries and making cross
references were being systematized, so also were those for preparing the entry proper. In the several rules Panizzi devoted to
the description of the book, he called for a brief but accurate transcription of the title and faithful recording of the edition, the number of volumes, and the place and date of publication.[63] Again,
there was no American statement in comparable detail describing
American practices; American libraries did, however, occasionally
exhibit a high regard for the wording of the title page. In the 1838
Andover catalogue, for example, Taylor declared: "I have never,
except ... for purposes of elucidation and abridgement, considered
myself at liberty to deviate from the titles."[64] The better American catalogues of the day were also in accord with Panizzi in the
preparation of the remainder of the book description.

Biographical and bibliographical notes beyond anything envi-
sioned in Panizzi's rules were added to the entries in several
American catalogues. In the 1838 Andover catalogue Taylor appended brief biographical notices to the names of the personal
authors. Revatus Maussuet, for example, was described as "a
Benedictine of the Congregation of St. Mauer; b. 1665. d. 1716";
Peter van Mastricht as "D.D. Prof. of Theol. Utrecht; b. 1630.
d. 1706"; and Increase Mather as "d.d. Presid. of Harvard College; b. 1639. d. 1723."[65] Once more Jewett followed the example
of his teacher, but on a less generous scale. In his 1843 Brown
University catalogue, Jewett limited the notices to authors having
the same name, to ancient authors, and to American authors. Such
information obviously went beyond that necessary for the catalogue
to serve as an index and tended to make of it a reference book.
Both catalogues also included frequent bibliographical notes.

The notes which Edward Johnston included in the 1837 catalogue of the New York Mercantile Library were more in the nature
of bibliographical essays. Appended to many of the subject groupings were lengthy paragraphs calling attention to those books not
present in the collections but judged of importance. In Johnston's
own words, "Such a series of indications was regarded as useful
towards shaping the future additions to the library, and as capable
of rendering the catalogue serviceable, as a book of reference and
a guide in reading...."[66] Typical of these notes was that which
appeared at the conclusion of the list of books on architecture:

In architecture, Vitruvius is the great ancient, and Palladio the chief modern master. Of the former, Schneider's edition, Leipsig, 1807, 3 vols. royal 8vo, and of the latter, the version of Scamozzi (French), Venice, 1796, 5 in 3 vols. 4to, are best. For a bibliography of the art, consult Loudon's Encyclopaedia of Architecture.[67]

Brief annotations were also appended to particular titles throughout the catalogue. Johnston's efforts in this catalogue are reminiscent of the superb annotations and bibliographical essays which Justin Winsor was to include in the catalogues of the Boston Public Library some forty years later. The ambitious purpose of both men was nothing less than to make their catalogues serve as reading guides. Thus, as the first half of the nineteenth century drew to a close, whatever other motives may have previously prompted the preparation of catalogues, a single purpose was now clearly dominant—to devise a tool that would assist the reader in his use of the library.

Chapter III

The Age of Jewett, 1850-1875: General Considerations

AMERICAN LIBRARIES AT MID-CENTURY

In the history of American libraries few developments were as dramatic as the rise of the free public library—established by state law, supported by local taxation, publicly controlled, and free to all citizens on the same terms. Although the conditions which brought this institution into being had long been in evolution, public libraries themselves did not appear until the third quarter of the nineteenth century. In 1849 the legislature of New Hampshire passed the first general law authorizing towns to tax themselves for the establishment and maintenance of libraries. New Hampshire's example was followed by Massachusetts in 1851, by Maine in 1854, and by others, until by 1875 most of the states had passed similar permissive legislation.

Towns and cities, particularly in Massachusetts and New Hampshire, promptly availed themselves of this opportunity for gaining public libraries; shortly, several large and important public libraries were in existence: notably, in Boston, Cincinnati, Chicago, and Louisville. In the free public library a type of institution finally evolved, after decades of experimentation, which proved to have both permanence and financial stability.

Because the public library corrected those precise ills—impermanence and financial instability—that had plagued the social library, the latter fell abruptly from favor. Although shortly before 1850 the social library was at its peak of development, by 1885, according to Jesse Hauk Shera, the "case against it as a library form was unmistakably clear."[1] Nor was this development unnoticed by the librarians of the day. Concerning the social library Frederic B. Perkins wrote in 1876 that "it does not now seem likely that many additional libraries will be joined to the existing class."[2] During this period the collections of many of the social libraries were either dissipated or merged with newly formed public libraries. In several of the larger cities, however, the mercantile libraries were well supported and firmly entrenched. The result was that in these cities—New York, Philadelphia, Brooklyn, San Francisco—the coming of the public library was delayed for some time.

This period also witnessed great progress in the establishment and growth of state libraries. In 1876, Henry A. Homes reported that every state and territory had its library, ten of which had more than 30,000 volumes.[3] Although the primary function of the state libraries was to serve their legislatures and courts, many had already been given the added responsibility for promoting library services throughout their areas.

The zeal to collect and preserve the materials of American history continued unabated; by 1876 there were more than seventy-five historical society libraries in the country.[4] Although many of them were small and insignificant, a few—the American Antiquarian Society and the New York, Massachusetts, and Wisconsin Historical societies—had excellent resources.

Another significant development was the establishment of the first great philanthropic libraries in America. Of prime importance was the library which the money of John Jacob Astor and the knowledge of Joseph Green Cogswell provided for the people of New York. From the first day the Astor opened its doors, it was in the front rank of American libraries. Notable libraries were also built by James Lenox in New York City and by George Peabody in Baltimore.

In American higher education the years between 1850 and 1875 were ones of transition. At mid-century the American college, with its classical curriculum inherited from colonial times, still held sway even though it was being challenged. Twenty-five years later, the founding of Johns Hopkins signaled the rise of the new American university. A series of advances combined to produce this remarkable change.

Prominent among them was the movement which ultimately gave scientific and technological instruction full status in the undergraduate college program. Because of the rigidity of the classical curriculum, the earlier technological schools were compelled to assume either an independent existence or the inferior status of an affiliate of a recognized college. The acceptance of these more utilitarian studies was hastened by action of the United States government. As a result of the Morrill Act of 1862, subsidies for instruction in technology and agriculture were available either to

the existing state universities or to the newly formed land-grant
colleges.

The professional schools, such as law and medicine, experienced similar difficulties. In their beginnings they had only the
most tenuous relationship, if any, with the established colleges;
however, as they were able to raise their level of instruction and
as their stature increased in the eyes of society, they gradually
gained full acceptance.

A movement which facilitated the acceptance of professional,
technological, and scientific studies—and, indeed, many other disciplines yet to appear—was the system of free election of courses
by students. Although curricular reforms leading toward free
election had been attempted at both the University of Virginia and
at Brown, and at Harvard in an earlier day, it remained for President Eliot of Harvard to complete the task.

Finally, there was the long struggle to incorporate graduate
studies into American higher education. For decades American
students in search of advanced training in the nonprofessional
fields of science and letters had been required to attend the great
German universities. Not surprisingly, the German influence was
strong in the first graduate programs instituted in America.

Curiously enough, these momentous changes in American institutions of higher education had little immediate effect upon their
libraries. Whereas the newly introduced graduate programs would
eventually revolutionize the character of American academic libraries, there was not time for this effect to be felt during the period under review.

GROWING IMPORTANCE OF LIBRARY CATALOGUES

During the third quarter of the nineteenth century both American libraries and their catalogues were dominated by the free public library movement. Few library officers and trustees failed to
realize the significance of the public library's dependence upon the
general citizenry for its establishment and for its continued support. The conception of the library as a service institution came
rapidly to the fore, and all conflicting ideas were critically examined. Chief among the determinants of library policies were the
desires and the convenience of the general reader. This was especially true in the compilation of library catalogues. The Trustees of the Boston Public Library spoke for all library trustees
when they stated in the preface to their 1861 catalogue that:

In preparing it, every other consideration has been made subordinate to the desire of rendering it practically useful—of

offering to our fellow citizens of all classes and conditions,
a simple, convenient manual, which shall make the books of
the Library and their contents easily and pleasantly accessible. No ideas of theoretical perfection in catalogues, either
as to form, as to extent, or as to any nice harmony in their
constituent parts, have been allowed to stand, for an instant,
in the way of this main purpose.[5]

Although there was agreement that the prime purpose of the
catalogue was to aid the reader in his use of the library, there
were many different opinions as to what this involved. Few librarians of the day questioned the necessity of the catalogue's in-
dicating which books were in the library; concerning the extent to
which the catalogue should reveal the subject content of these
books, however, there was complete lack of accord. Although
Jewett prepared an excellent alphabetical index of subjects for the
1843 Brown University catalogue, ten years later he was of the belief that readers seldom came to libraries in search of books on
particular subjects:

> The experience of all students, of all who use books, if
> carefully noted, will show, that, in a vast majority of cases,
> whoever wishes to refer to books in a library, knows the
> names of their authors. It follows, that this form of arrange-
> ment must be, in the main, the most convenient; and if any
> other be pursued, it can but accommodate the minority, at the
> expense of the majority.[6]

Joseph Green Cogswell, who shared Jewett's doubts concerning the
value of the subject catalogue, was convinced that any use it had
was for those unfamiliar with books and reading.[7] With both points
—the frequency with which readers resorted to the subject approach, and its use only by those unacquainted with books—Cutter
took issue:

> Leaving the desultory readers out of the question, half the
> people who go to libraries have no author or book in their
> minds; they have a question to look up, and the library is
> useless to them unless they can find out in some way who has
> written upon that question.[8]

As to whether those accustomed to using books found it necessary
to use the subject approach, Cutter noted that:

> Even professors find it no easy task to notice all the books
> that appear in their own line of study, to remember them all,
> and to have the authors' names at their tongues' end, as he
> must do who consults a library provided only with an

author-catalogue. Moreover, scholars often want to look up some matter outside of their habitual course of study; with merely an author-catalogue they are entirely adrift....[9]

Another argument frequently advanced by opponents of subject catalogues was that "the European libraries possess either very imperfect subject-catalogues or none at all, because this task belongs to the bibliographer."[10] To this Cutter replied:

> The objections to giving up subject-catalogues in libraries and substituting bibliographies are, first, the non-existence of the bibliographies; second, the incompleteness of such bibliographies as there are; third, the fact that bibliographies "begin to be imperfect even before they are published"; and fourth, the inconvenience of using them even if complete and brought down to date.[11]

Nor did Cutter believe that librarians were capable of either replacing the subject catalogue or getting along without it:

> It [the subject catalogue] is costly, but it is cheaper than men and women intelligent and learned enough to be its substitutes, and it does not die or get married as men and women do; it is never tired and forgetful; it requires no vacations, and is never sick. But more than all this is the fact that these male and female attendants, however bright they may be, find that when resort is made to them by readers they absolutely need its assistance to enable them to give information satisfactory either to themselves or to the questioners.[12]

By 1875, Cutter's views had prevailed. The complete catalogue, most librarians would have agreed, must give information concerning the author, title, and subject of every book in the library, and many librarians would have added parts of certain books and articles in selected periodicals. The task laid out for the catalogue was formidable, and it was to be accomplished with a minimum of assistance from printed bibliographies and from librarians.

ADVANTAGES OF THE PRINTED BOOK CATALOGUE

When librarians thought of their ideal catalogue at the end of the third quarter of the nineteenth century—as, indeed, when they had thought of it at the beginning and at the mid-point of the century—they saw it printed and in book form. This was not because these librarians were unaware of the difficulties of printing. In 1876, Justin Winsor, only five years after he had been forced to abandon the printed book catalogue in favor of the card catalogue at the Boston Public Library, wrote that "the printing of a catalogue is a great expense to a library, but it is a necessary one for a popular library."[13] He felt constrained to add, however, that "a large library seldom prints more than one."

William F. Poole, after having been thwarted for several years in his efforts to print something more than brief finding lists for the collections of the Chicago Public Library, still insisted in 1877 that until a complete catalogue of the library was printed, "the full resources of the Library ... will not be accessible, nor its value for reference appreciated."[14] In 1876, Cutter, struggling with the great catalogue of the Boston Athenaeum which was to strain severely the resources of that institution before it was completed, still advised his colleagues that "if there is money specially intended for printing, or if money can be obtained for this purpose, without diminishing the funds for the purchase of books, by all means print."[15]

What were the great attractions of the printed book catalogues which caused the ablest of librarians to persist in their determination to print? They consisted, it would appear, of certain advantages inherent in the printed catalogue itself and of the absence of any really acceptable substitute form.

The obvious and perhaps greatest advantage of the printed book catalogue was that it was in print. The only alternative to print at the time was, of course, manuscript. Typewriters were not commercially produced before the close of this period, and they were not employed generally in libraries until several years later. The early inclusion of courses in the "library hand" in the new library schools was eloquent testimony of the concern libraries felt for manuscript. To avoid handwriting in his new card catalogue of the Boston Public Library, Justin Winsor in 1872 instituted the practice in America of printing titles on thin sheets of paper, which were later cut and pasted upon cards.[16] The printed page also permitted several titles to be viewed at the same time, whereas the card catalogue allowed but one title to be seen without flipping a card.

Another advantage of the printed book catalogue was that any desired number of copies could be made available in the library at little additional cost. Fifty copies of the printed catalogue of the Lawrence, Massachusetts, Free Public Library, for example, were available in the Library at all times.[17] Any comparable duplication of manuscript catalogues was, of course, out of the question.

Much importance was attached also to the fact that the printed catalogue could be consulted outside the library. For noncirculating libraries, and for the college libraries which were easily accessible to students and faculty, this was an advantage of limited value. Among the general circulating libraries, however, the New Bedford Public Library probably summed up the sentiment: "Almost every family in the city, any of whose members enjoyed the privileges of the Library, would feel a work of this kind to be indispensable to its profitable use."[18] The difficulties encountered by libraries in efforts to sell copies of their catalogues would seem to contradict this statement; however, it could be argued that the cost of the catalogues was the deterring factor since Poole, when he was able to offer brief finding lists to the people of Chicago for ten or fifteen cents, sold thousands of copies.[19] As for the value of the catalogue of one library in others, one is again confronted with the fact that few catalogues found their way into libraries other than as gifts. There were notable exceptions, such as the catalogues of the Brooklyn Library and the Boston Athenaeum, which were found in libraries throughout the country.[20]

A final attraction of the printed catalogue was tradition—librarians had been accustomed to seeing their catalogues in this form for over two hundred years. This practice, which became entrenched during a time when catalogues were small and simple to print, was difficult to discontinue even though the nature and cost of catalogues had changed radically.

PROBLEMS OF PRINTING

Several developments occurred in libraries during this period which greatly increased the costs of compiling and printing catalogues. There was, for example, a marked expansion in the function of the catalogue. An adequate and satisfactory catalogue, it was decided, must not only list the books in the library, but also describe their contents in detail. At the same time that the catalogue was asked to broaden its objectives, it was also required to include new books in unprecedented numbers. To keep the printed book catalogue up-to-date without resorting either to innumerable supplements or to frequent reprintings of the entire catalogue was a Herculean assignment. Its accomplishment was not made easier by the inadequate library budgets of the day. Money which was badly needed for books and other library purposes was given over grudgingly for the preparation and printing of catalogues. And, unfortunately, it was necessary to charge the expense of printing largely against the general library funds. Despite the great popularity of the printed book catalogue, readers were noticeably reluctant to purchase copies.

By the end of this period the costs of compiling and printing

had become so burdensome that the great majority of libraries
were compelled to abandon the printed catalogue in book form. Of
the one hundred libraries in the United States in 1875 with collections exceeding 20,000 volumes, only two fifths had printed complete book catalogues within the previous quarter century, and only
one fourth within the previous five years.[21] The stronghold of the
printed catalogue was among the state libraries. All but one of the
fourteen state libraries with collections in excess of 20,000 volumes had published catalogues during the previous twenty-five
years, and all but four within the previous five years.[22] During
this same period, 1850-1875, the academic libraries had all but
abandoned the printed book catalogue. Of the thirty-five college
libraries with over 20,000 volumes, only nine had published catalogues after 1850, and only four after 1870.[23] The difficulties
which compelled librarians to give up the printed book catalogue
are discussed in detail below.

Addition of the Subject Approach to Catalogues

Nothing was more instrumental in the retreat of the printed
book catalogue than the decision that it should describe the subject
content of the books in the collection. For the printed catalogue
the ensuing multiplication of entries proved to be disastrous. Until
well into the nineteenth century, it will be recalled, catalogues
rarely had more than one entry for each title, at which time the
better catalogues gradually came to be provided with indexes: alphabetical indexes of authors for the classified catalogues, broadly
classified subject indexes for the alphabetical author catalogues.
The addition of indexes resulted in considerable increase in the
size of the catalogues. What really swelled the catalogues, however, was the advent of the dictionary arrangement, with its multiple entries for the same book under author, title, and subject.

The size of catalogues was also increased by the practice of
preparing entries for parts of books and for articles in encyclopedias and periodicals. An example in point was the 1875 catalogue
of the Quincy, Massachusetts, Public Library, which listed only
7,000 volumes but contained no fewer than 4,000 entries for articles in periodicals.[24] A few catalogues, notably those of the Boston and Quincy Public libraries, even contained annotations for
many individual titles and bibliographic essays for several subjects.[25]

The effect of the above practices upon the size of the catalogues is dramatically shown by a comparison of the 1864 Library
of Congress catalogue,[26] which was a simple alphabetical author
listing, with the 1874-82 Boston Athenaeum catalogue,[27] which was

a model of the full dictionary arrangement. Both catalogues indexed collections of about 90,000 volumes, both had full entries set in small type, and both were arranged in double columns. The Library of Congress catalogue was but 1,236 pages in length; the Boston Athenaeum catalogue was 3,400 pages, nearly three times as long.

Growth of Library Collections

Also contributing to the problems of the printed book catalogue was the rapidly increasing size of library collections. In 1849, Jewett found in all of America not one library collection of 100,000 volumes, only five of over 50,000, and but nine with over 25,000 volumes.[28] One quarter of a century later, ten libraries reported over 100,000 volumes, twenty over 50,000 volumes, and one hundred over 25,000 volumes.[29] The rate of growth of collections was even more startling. In 1875 the "Average Yearly Additions" reported by the ten largest libraries in the country was 8,000-10,000 volumes.[30] At this rate of growth, a library beginning with nothing would have had more books in just ten years than the largest library in the land had at the middle of the nineteenth century.

Libraries attempted valiantly to keep their printed catalogues abreast of these swelling book collections. In 1861 the Library of Congress published a classified catalogue of its 70,000-volume collection.[31] The addition of 15,000 volumes in the next three years called forth another catalogue in 1864—this time an alphabetical author catalogue.[32] Five years later, with the acquisition of 25,000 more volumes, an alphabetico-classed catalogue was published—the third completely redone catalogue of the entire collection in a period of nine years.[33]

Most libraries, not possessing financial resources comparable to those of the Congressional library, were unable to print complete catalogues every few years. The consequence, of course, was that their catalogues fell rapidly into arrears. In 1866, just five years after Jewett had completed his excellent catalogue of the Upper Hall of the Boston Public Library, 34,000 additional volumes had accumulated.[34] The catalogue of the Boston Athenaeum, after having been in preparation for over twenty years, was finally completed in 1882; it contained, however, no book that had been added in the ten years immediately preceding the publication of the final volume.[35] In 1891, less than ten years after the completion of the catalogue, the collections of the Athenaeum exceeded 173,000 volumes.[36] Only about 90,000 of these were listed in the printed catalogue.

Cost of Publishing Book Catalogues

Another formidable obstacle to printing catalogues was cost.
To many an administrator the problem must have appeared insolu-
ble. Even if a moderately sized edition were sold, the cost per
copy would have been considerable. Actually, of course, readers
were noticeably reluctant to buy copies, which forced the price
still higher. Also, the stock of unsold copies declined sharply in
value as new books were added to the collections which were not
listed in the catalogue.

Figures for the cost of preparing copy for the catalogues are
particularly elusive. In most instances the work was done by regular employees in addition to their other duties and with no separate accounting of time. Too, there is the problem of deciding how
much of the cataloguing work was occasioned by the intention to
print and how much would have been necessary in any event. One
fact, however, is painfully evident—the amount of work involved
was substantial and usually far exceeded that which was antici-
pated. The experience of Alfred Whitaker in preparing the 1874
catalogue of the San Francisco Mercantile Library was typical:

> It seems ludicrous on looking back, to see how wide from
> the mark many of the estimates were. We were led to expect
> that nine months would end the work of preparation, and we
> based all our calculations upon a book of five hundred pages.
> It took two years to prepare the copy, and the volume swelled
> as the work progressed, until it reached nearly one thousand
> pages.[37]

It is to be hoped that no catalogue of this period consumed
more time in its preparation than the excellent one of the Boston
Athenaeum. It had been in process for several years when Charles
R. Lowell arrived in Boston in 1862 to take over its direction. Upon his death eight years later Cutter assumed control, and four
more years elapsed before the first volume appeared. Not until
1882, eight years later, was the catalogue completed. During a
large part of this time from two to eight persons were working upon it. It is estimated that $100,000 was required to bring this cat-
alogue into print, of which about $80,000 was for preparation and
only about $20,000 for setting type, paper, printing, binding, and
the like.[38] No one took issue with Dewey when he warned his colleagues that "for preparing the copy a much greater outlay in sal-
aries"[39] was necessary than for printing.

The cost of printing individual catalogues can be determined
somewhat more accurately. The San Francisco Mercantile Library, for example, spent $8,087.31 for the printing of its full

dictionary catalogue in 1874, [40] a sum which was over half of the library's expenditures for all other purposes that year and which exceeded by $1,500 the amount spent for books. [41] During one of the years (1874-75) that the $100,000 catalogue of the Boston Athenaeum was being prepared, the expenditures of that institution for all other purposes amounted to only $32,663. [42] From the foregoing examples the burden of printing a complete catalogue every few years is distressingly apparent.

Limited Sales of Catalogues

At this point one might ask why the printing of a catalogue was always regarded as an expense. Could not the money expended for publication be regained through the sale of copies, thus making the catalogue self-supporting? The value of the printed book catalogue to readers was greatly reduced, Winsor believed, by its inability to include books added subsequent to its publication. [43] These recently acquired volumes were, of course, most frequently sought by users. Cutter felt that in a college library the catalogue in printed form provided small advantage since students and faculty resided close to the library. For the large circulating libraries, especially in the cities, he saw considerably more use for the printed catalogue; however, even for these libraries he had doubts, for he observed that in several such libraries that had published catalogues in recent years, the sale of catalogues had been small. [44] Poole, too, had been disillusioned concerning the number of copies of a catalogue that the public would buy. "Its chief use," he wrote, "will be by readers and book borrowers in the library, and for exchange with other libraries." [45]

In June of 1875, Cutter directed a questionnaire to seventy-five libraries that had recently published catalogues. There was little in the responses of the institutions to challenge either his opinions or those of Winsor and Poole. The majority of the libraries had issued their catalogues in editions of less than 1,000 copies, and only three—Boston Public Library, Astor Library, and the Pennsylvania State Library—in editions of as many as 3,000 copies. Unfortunately, these small editions proved to be more than adequate. The majority of the libraries did not succeed in selling even 100 copies, and only two libraries—Philadelphia Mercantile and San Francisco Mercantile—sold as many as 900 copies. [46]

Still fewer catalogues would have been sold had libraries offered them to their readers at full cost. "We have pursued the policy at Boston," wrote Winsor, "of attaching only such a price to our catalogues as will prevent waste." [47] He cited as an example their recently published catalogue of the Roxbury Branch. Although a copy had cost $1.25 to print, it was sold for thirty cents. Most libraries, unable to be so generous, were obliged to charge a price somewhat higher. The Springfield City Library Association sold copies of their catalogue for $2—about half its cost.[48] Worcester Free Public Library sold for twenty-five cents copies of a catalogue which cost fifty-five cents to print.[49]

The librarians of the day could hardly have escaped the observation that serious financial losses almost invariably attended the printing of a catalogue. "In the publication of catalogues," wrote Whitaker, "this is the universal experience."[50] The effort to defend these losses and to vindicate publication called forth many an eloquent testimony on the value of the printed catalogue. Whitaker summarized the sentiment well:

> To such as look upon its [the catalogue's] issue, however, as a publisher upon his latest venture, and see nothing beyond the coin amount realized from the sale of copies, it must ever seem a failure; but to the users of books, the general reader, the student, or the importunate reference hunter; to other libraries, among which it has been generously distributed, and to all the liberally inclined, it will be welcomed as an indispensable adjunct of the Library itself, and a not unprofitable contribution to the field of bibliography.[51]

ALTERNATIVES TO THE FULL PRINTED CATALOGUE IN BOOK FORM

Reluctant to forego printing entirely, libraries experimented with numerous substitutes for the full printed catalogue. Adopted with varying degrees of success were the traditional supplements to the full printed catalogues; periodically issued bulletins of current acquisitions; lists of current acquisitions published in newspapers; catalogues of particular classes within the collections; and condensed lists and indexes to be used in conjunction with card catalogues. Finally, there was the carefully conceived plan of Jewett to stereotype catalogues at the Smithsonian Institution for individual libraries.

Supplements

The printing of supplements for general catalogues did not originate in this period. In fact, the first library catalogue published in America—the 1723 catalogue of Harvard College—had supplements printed in 1725 and 1735.[52] The usual practice was

to construct these supplements, containing the acquisitions of up to
ten years, upon the same plan as the parent catalogue. Although
this temporarily avoided the necessity of redoing the entire catalogue, it was not an entirely satisfactory solution and even created
a new problem—the proliferation of supplements. Cutter believed
that the average reader would not search through more than three
or four supplements and that even the most serious readers would
be reluctant to go beyond six.[53] At this point, then, it was necessary for the entire catalogue to be rearranged and reprinted. As
collections increased in size, even the wealthiest libraries found
this procedure burdensome, and eventually intolerable. Libraries
were confronted with the choice either of ceasing to print, as their
European counterparts had done, or of finding a new solution.

Jewett's Stereotyped Catalogue

In the mind of Jewett a scheme for resolving the printing impasse had been maturing for several years. Jewett was particularly struck with the expense incurred by libraries across the land
in preparing entries for the same books. He estimated that in any
two general libraries with over 10,000 volumes, at least one quarter of the titles were the same. Upon examination of the Smithsonian's collection of public library catalogues, he offered the
further observation that of the 450,000 entries they collectively
contained, not more than 150,000 were for different titles.[54] In the
elimination of this duplication of effort, Jewett reasoned, lay the
salvation of the printed catalogue. How work once done could be
utilized in the preparation of future catalogues was clearly the
problem.

Jewett proposed to accomplish this through the preparation of
a separate stereotype plate for each title. Once made, these plates
could be used repeatedly for different catalogues. The plates were
to be retained at the Institution, where all printing was to be done.
Thus, a library desiring to have a catalogue of its collections made
would be permitted free use of all stereotype plates in the posses-
sion of the Smithsonian, and would be charged only for the assembly and redistribution of the plates which were used, for the
composition of plates for new titles, and for the presswork.
Avoided would be the cost of composition, with the attendant costs
of revision and correction, for all titles except those new to the
system.

An integral part of Jewett's plan was the preparation of a set
of "Rules for Preparing Catalogues" which would govern the cataloguing of all cooperating libraries.[55] Only in this manner, of
course, could entries prepared in different libraries be combined

in the same catalogue. These uniform rules would also make possible the preparation of a general catalogue of American libraries
—the first step, Jewett dared to hope, "towards the accomplishment of that cherished dream of scholars, a universal catalogue."[56]

Despite its failure Jewett's scheme was carefully conceived
and endorsed by the highest authorities of the day. Jewett himself
had the plan under consideration for over three years before he
announced it publicly in 1850 at the New Haven meeting of the
American Association for the Advancement of Science.[57] A short
time later, the Smithsonian Institution retained a Commission
composed of six of the most eminent librarians and literary men
of the day to pass judgment upon the practicability of Jewett's
plan, including his cataloguing rules. In their report the Commis-
sioners expressed belief "that the plan in all its parts is practicable" and that the cataloguing rules were "drawn up with judgment
and care." [58]

The Librarians' Conference of 1853 heard Jewett present his
plan in detail and passed several approving resolutions.[59] Individual libraries were also impressed with the plan. In 1855 the
American Antiquarian Society postponed the publication of its catalogue for two or three years in the hope that by that time Jewett's
plan would be in operation.[60] Nevertheless, Jewett's hopes were
never realized, partly because he was compelled to sever his con-
nections with the Smithsonian in 1854, and partly because the materials he selected for his stereotype plates presented serious
technical difficulties. Librarians were thus forced to turn from
Jewett's grand and sweeping scheme, and to seek release from
their catalogue problems in other less-spectacular ways.

Condensed Catalogues

In 1854 librarians were heartened by the appearance of two
catalogues in Boston which seemed to offer, by virtue of their
simplicity and brevity, a measure of relief from the oppressive
printing costs. One of the catalogues was prepared for the new
Boston Public Library by Edward Capen, its first librarian;[61] the
other, for the Boston Mercantile Library by William F. Poole.[62]
The Public Library catalogue was a simple author listing with
very brief entries, consisting of the author's surname and initials,
short title, date of publication, and book location number—usually
all on a single line. Its significance was obviously not in any innovation of form; rather, it lay in the thinking that prompted its
preparation.

The staff of the Library had prepared for their own use in
helping readers a full alphabetical card catalogue containing

entries under authors and all likely words in the titles. This card catalogue, the Trustees believed, constituted "the best basis for a thorough knowledge of the Library by the Librarian and his assistants, and for the use of its books by all persons who wish to make careful investigation of particular subjects."[63] With this excellent card catalogue at hand the Trustees felt that the simplest sort of printed list would suffice—one that would merely list the volumes in the library by author, with their locations.

Such an arrangement—a full catalogue on cards supplemented by the simple printed list of the library's holdings—appealed to librarians of that day for a number of reasons. In order to maintain records of their current additions, most of the libraries had already developed card catalogues. At the same time many of them had been unable to publish full printed catalogues, but they still believed that some sort of a printed list was highly desirable. Accordingly, libraries found the practice of the Boston Public Library both reasonable and attractive, and many of them followed the example in the ensuing years.

In addition to popularizing the dictionary arrangement, Poole's 1854 catalogue for the Boston Mercantile Library demonstrated that a serviceable list could be compiled and printed at a fairly low cost. Poole combined in a single alphabetical sequence both author and subject-word entries. By the use of short titles and authors' initials rather than forenames, the entries were held to a line in length. Further economies were effected by omitting cross references and by keeping contents notes and entries for parts of books to a minimum. Such a catalogue was obviously economical of space and easy of compilation; at the same time, it was surprisingly useful.

The entire cost of this catalogue in an edition of 3,000 copies amounted to only $1,736.26, which included payments for the extra services of the librarian and a temporary assistant as well as for the paper, printing, and the binding of 600 copies.[64] This amount of money would not have paid the costs of printing alone for a full catalogue of a comparably sized library. In many quarters Poole's catalogue was regarded as the answer to the burdensome costs of compiling and printing catalogues. In the years that followed, it served as the model for several new catalogues: Cincinnati Young Men's Mercantile Library in 1855, Philadelphia Mercantile Library in 1856, and the Brooklyn Mercantile and New Bedford Free Public libraries in 1858.[65]

Catalogues Published in Parts

Although the printed catalogue in condensed form and designed to be supplemented by a full catalogue on cards reduced substantially the costs of compilation and printing, some libraries preferred an alternate scheme—the printing of the catalogue in several independent parts at varying times rather than as a whole and at a single time. The parts were usually, although not always, catalogues of the books in a single class of literature and were appropriately termed "class lists." This plan possessed several advantages. Although the printing of a catalogue in parts rather than as a whole represented no over-all saving, it did permit libraries to spread the expense over a period of years.

It also permitted considerable flexibility in the frequency of reprintings and in the size of editions. The class lists for those portions of the collection that were growing rapidly could be quickly and easily reprinted without the necessity of reworking the entire catalogue. At the same time it was possible to vary the size of the editions from one class list to another according to the expected use and sales. Finally, individuals could obtain catalogues of those parts of the collection that particularly interested them without being put to the expense of purchasing a catalogue of the entire collection.

It seems likely that the origin of the "class list" lay in the heavy reading of fictional works by patrons of the early nineteenth-century libraries. The catalogues frequently provided separate listings for fiction as, for example, that published by the New York Mercantile Library in 1844.[66] Eventually these fictional lists came to be published separately. It remained, however, for Joseph Green Cogswell to see the full possibilities of the publication of a catalogue in parts. In his annual report in 1854 as Superintendent of the Astor Library, he described his plan "to take up the library by departments and prepare a classed catalogue, to be printed as each department is completed."[67] Before Cogswell was forced to abandon this scheme in favor of an alphabetical catalogue of the entire collection, he did succeed in publishing a lithographed edition of the oriental books in 100 copies.[68]

As was the case with so many cataloguing innovations during the last half of the nineteenth century, the Boston Public Library first demonstrated the practicability of issuing a catalogue in parts. By 1866, eight years had elapsed since a complete catalogue, or even a supplement, of the rapidly growing Lower Hall circulating collection had been published. In that year the officials, doubting the wisdom of diverting from the purchase of books sufficient funds to prepare a full catalogue, decided to issue a series of brief class lists of the more heavily used portions of the Lower Hall collections. During the first year, lists were published of the books in three areas: fiction; history and politics; and theology, medicine, and law. A list of the French, German, and Italian works appeared in 1867, and a list of the biographical and travel books in 1868. Two years later, in 1870, a miscellaneous list was printed of the works in poetry, drama, rhetoric, elocution, and the like, and of the periodicals.[69] In the next two or three decades these six class lists were reprinted repeatedly and were joined by several additional lists of other classes of literature.

Library Bulletins

The observation that library patrons were interested primarily in the latest books on their particular subjects of inquiry led several librarians, at about this time, to suspect that the usual methods of printing catalogues could never furnish the immediate communication with readers that was desired. That the catalogues might be condensed rather than full, and issued in parts rather than as a whole, did not seem to change the situation materially. Their proposed solution, logically, was to keep the public informed by issuing promptly and at frequent intervals lists of recently added books—"library bulletins," as they came to be known. The bulletin was also viewed as a means of publicizing library announcements, communicating library policies to readers, and making available bibliographies on special subjects, especially ones of current interest. The bulletins were usually published quarterly, although sometimes more frequently, and were distributed to readers either free of charge or for a few cents. The entries, only one for each book, were sparing of bibliographical detail and arranged, in most instances, alphabetically by author.

For this innovation the library world was once more indebted to that seemingly inexhaustible source of new cataloguing ideas—the Boston Public Library. In 1866, the Examining Committee, wearied by efforts to keep their catalogues current, recommended that the library seek a readier means of communication with its patrons.[70] Winsor's answer was the publication of the first issue of the quarterly bulletin in October, 1867.[71] It was a simple listing of the recent additions to all divisions of the library with each title appearing but once. The arrangement of the entries was alphabetically by author, except in the fourteenth through the sixteenth issues when a classed arrangement was tried. After 1872 the bulletins carried numerous special bibliographies, especially on timely subjects.

In his annual report for 1868, Winsor wrote:

> Our printed bulletins have been a success. They have been eagerly welcomed by our frequenters; greatly valued by other institutions; and I have received very laudatory opinions of them from accomplished librarians in Europe.[72]

His enthusiasm does not appear to have been unjustified. In 1869 the Boston Athenaeum followed his example and began issuing a bimonthly list of their recent acquisitions. [73] By 1876 the success of the library bulletin was assured. The public libraries of Concord, Lawrence, New Bedford, and Worcester in Massachusetts; the Peabody Institute; the Peoria, Illinois, Mercantile Library; and the Dennis Library in Newton, New Jersey, were all supplying their patrons with similar lists of new books. [74]

BEGINNINGS OF THE PUBLIC CARD CATALOGUE

A curious feature of the printed book catalogue was that its very nature required the existence of a supplementary catalogue in a different physical form. In even the wealthiest and best-managed libraries a considerable period of time elapsed between the successive printings of catalogues. It was to make available these books which were added to the library in this interval between printings that the card catalogue owes, at least in part, its origin and growth in American libraries.

The use of slips of paper, or cards, for the recording of information concerning books was far from a novelty in American libraries in 1850. In preparing copy for their printed catalogues, librarians had long since discovered the usefulness of transcribing individual entries for books upon cards, which could then be interfiled, arranged, and rearranged to suit their various purposes. Upon the completion of the printing of the catalogue, these slips, which were frequently fuller in description than the corresponding entries in the printed catalogue, were customarily placed in boxes and retained for reference purposes. As additional books were added to the library, entries for these volumes were recorded on cards, which were then either interfiled in the main sequence of cards or filed separately as a supplement. The record thus formed possessed a double value. According to Poole, until such time as a new catalogue could be printed, these cards, together with the old catalogue, furnished a record of the holdings of the library "complete up to the latest book received." [75] At the same time the ultimate in preparedness for a new printed catalogue was achieved, since the cards stood "in readiness to be put to press at any moment."

For several reasons card catalogues were at first available to the patrons of the library only through the intermediary of the librarian. Since the cards themselves were intended as "copy" for any future catalogues that might be printed, librarians understandably were reluctant to permit their unsupervised use. The primitive catalogue-drawer assembly contributed to the librarians' misgivings concerning the use of the cards by the public generally. Means of insuring that the cards would not be misfiled, removed, or stolen were still unperfected. So, too, were guide cards, follower blocks, and other devices which would eventually facilitate the use of cards. Finally, the cards were in manuscript and in a relatively unfamiliar form. In the words of Cogswell, "such a catalogue is, of course, only fit for the use of the officers of the Library."[76] Many library patrons were inclined to agree. The *Boston Transcript* professed to speak for all of them when it stated:

> It is not necessary to describe a "card catalogue," since every frequenter of any library ... in which it is in use knows to his sorrow exactly what it is, and that it has wasted more of his time in the invention of becoming epithets in its condemnation than he has given to the books consulted through its use.[77]

As the difficulties of printing book catalogues mounted, and as improvements were made in the physical card catalogue assembly, librarians gradually became more disposed to grant their readers the direct use of the card catalogue. Although favored individuals had probably long been permitted to thumb through the cards on occasion, it was not until the 1850's that the first libraries opened their card catalogues to their readers at large.[78] One of the first and most widely acclaimed public card catalogues was that instituted at Harvard in 1861 by Ezra Abbot, with the assistance of young Cutter. In discussing this catalogue in 1863, Abbot commented that "the great advantage of keeping the alphabetical catalogue of a rapidly growing library on cards ... is now generally acknowledged."[79]

One of the last, significant objections to the card catalogue— its manuscript nature—was attacked at the Boston Public Library in 1872 by Justin Winsor. His plan, drawn from the example of Leyden University, was to print upon thin sheets of paper several entries which were then cut apart and pasted onto cards.[80] At about this time the St. Louis Public School Library also adopted the plan.[81]

As a result of the above-described and other improvements in card catalogues, Cutter felt justified in 1876 in urging his colleagues to "see if you cannot educate your people to use that [the card catalogue] and to get full as much good from it as they would from printed pages."[82] If Robinson's assessment of the advance of the card catalogue at the end of the third quarter of the nineteenth century is correct, a great many librarians were in accord with Cutter:

In some of the largest libraries of the country the card system has been exclusively adopted. Several of them have no
intention of printing any more catalogues in book form. In
others, cards are adopted for current accessions, with the
expectation of printing supplements from them, from time to
time. I think the tendency of the smaller libraries is to adopt
the former plan, keeping a manuscript card catalogue of books
as they are added, without a thought of printing.[83]

Thus, however much it may have been regretted in some quarters,
it was apparent to all, as the period drew to a close, that time was
fast running out for the full printed catalogue.

Chapter IV

The Age of Jewett, 1850-1875: Catalogue Arrangement

The growing insistence for an approach to the subject content of books, the difficulty of maintaining up-to-date printed lists of rapidly growing collections, the development of the public card catalogue, the high costs of preparing and printing catalogues, and the inadequate funds available to libraries generally—these were the factors shaping the arrangement of library catalogues in the third quarter of the nineteenth century. Both the traditional author catalogue and the traditional broadly classed catalogue proved to be ill-adapted for the increasing subject approach and for rapidly growing collections.

Librarians, in their efforts to devise a catalogue that could adjust to the new conditions, experimented with various arrangements. Basically, however, the arrangements were of two types—classified or dictionary—which set the stage for the classic struggle between the adherents of the two systems. Rightly or wrongly, the views of Cutter and the other proponents of the dictionary plan eventually prevailed over those of Dewey and his colleagues who supported the classified arrangement.

THE CLASSIFIED ARRANGEMENT

The Broadly Classed Catalogue

Although the broadly classed catalogue was employed rarely in America even in colonial times,[1] it had been used in Europe since medieval days. Early in the nineteenth century American librarians finally decided that their catalogues, too, should provide some indication of subject. Accordingly, they began to employ the only method known at that time for accomplishing this purpose—the

broadly classed catalogue. The first classed catalogues in America grouped the books alphabetically by author under several broad
subjects, without subdivision. Typical were the Boston Athenaeum
catalogue of 1810 which had fifteen classes,[2] the Charleston Library Society catalogue of 1811 with its seventeen classes,[3] and
the Library of Congress catalogue of 1812 with nineteen classes.[4]
Considering the modest size of collections of that day and the limited extent of the subject analysis needed, these catalogues probably functioned satisfactorily. Books were brought together into
broad subject groupings, with related groupings placed adjacent.
At the same time, the classification was still sufficiently simple to
permit the ready finding of an individual volume; it was merely
looked for under the appropriate class.

The Closely Classed Catalogue with Subdivisions

As collections became larger and the need for the subject approach more pressing, librarians adopted the practice of subdivid-
ing the various subject classes in their catalogues. One of the first
classed catalogues to employ subdivision on a generous scale was
that prepared for Yale in 1791.[5] Approximately 2,700 volumes
were grouped under sixteen classes which, jointly, had some forty
subdivisions. The proliferation of classes and subclasses reached
a climax in 1861, when the Library of Congress published a catalogue of its 70,000-volume collection in which the entries were
distributed among 179 sequences. The consequences of this multiplication of classes and subclasses were dire. As a finding list
for individual volumes, the classed catalogue with its multiple al-
phabets was of limited use. More often than not there was genuine
confusion as to which of several sequences should logically contain
a particular book. The abundance of sequences also complicated
the search for material on any given subject.

The Classed Catalogue with an Alphabetical Index of Authors

Librarians quickly discovered a solution for the first of the
above problems—that of locating an individual book. As early as
1789 the Library Company of Philadelphia appended to their
classed catalogue an index of authors' names. The index entry
took the form of the author's surname, followed by a reference to
the page in the classified portion of the catalogue where the entry
appeared in full. In 1815 the Library of Congress followed the
Library Company's example. Shortly, the practice of attaching
author indexes to classed catalogues was widely adopted. Catalogues were prepared according to this plan by the American

Philosophical Society in 1824, the Charleston Library Society in 1826, University of Pennsylvania in 1829,[6] the Philadelphia Library Company in 1835,[7] and the New York Mercantile Library in 1837, to name a few. The indexes in some of the later catalogues were considerably improved. In the 1835 Philadelphia Library Company catalogue, for example, the index provided fuller entries and was broadened to include anonymous works.

Upon occasion the foregoing arrangement was reversed, with the author sequence comprising the main portion of the catalogue and the classified arrangement forming an index. The catalogues prepared by the Library Company of Philadelphia in 1807, Harvard in 1830, and the New York Society Library in 1838[8] were examples. Either of the preceding catalogue arrangements, when properly executed, enabled the reader to locate readily a particular book; neither, however, eased his problem of finding a particular subject in increasingly complex classification schedules.

The Catalogue with Alphabetically Arranged Classes

Although logical classification was the chief means for exhibiting the subject content of libraries until about 1850, librarians had upon occasion arranged the classes in their catalogues alphabetically rather than according to one of the various philosophical systems. This arrangement was first employed in America in 1790. In that year Harvard College printed a catalogue in which the entries were arranged alphabetically by author under sixty-four classes which, in turn, were alphabetically arranged. In 1809 the Baltimore Library Company adopted the same alphabetical arrangement for the sixty classes in its catalogue. Bowdoin followed suit in 1821 for its catalogue of some thirty classes. The above catalogues contained more sequences than were usually found in the classed catalogues of the day. For this reason it can probably be assumed that the classes were deliberately arranged alphabetically, rather than logically, to facilitate the ready finding of particular subjects.

The monopoly of logical classification for the description of the subject content of library collections came to an abrupt end in 1843 with the appearance of Jewett's catalogue of the Brown University Library. As noted on page 28, Jewett appended to the author portion of his catalogue an alphabetically arranged index of subjects. In preparing this index, Jewett was quite aware that he was departing from accepted practices. "I cannot but think," he wrote, "[that the index] ... here offered will be found more convenient to the class of persons, who will use this library, than if it had been arranged according to any of the bibliographical systems, which have been proposed."[9]

Specifically, Jewett prepared for each book a subject entry which was taken directly from some word in the title, although occasionally he did form subject headings independently of the title. He then arranged these subject entries in one large alphabetical sequence, rather than grouping them according to some philosophical system of knowledge.

The appearance of Jewett's alphabetical index of subjects not only provided another means of describing the contents of books, but it also hastened improvements in the existing classed catalogue. Now that an alternative to logical classification was available, librarians were more inclined to examine their classed catalogues critically. The old argument that the student would "learn the philosophy of the universe while engaged in the simple occupation of hunting for a book"[10] soon came to be viewed skeptically. Librarians shortly realized that the real advantage of the classed catalogue was for the reader engaged in the systematic study of a particular topic. Brought together for him in one part of the catalogue were not only the books on his immediate subject but also the books on closely allied subjects, many of which might suggest new relationships to him. As he referred repeatedly to the same portion of the catalogue, he acquired a familiarity with it and eventually used it with ease and to advantage.

For the user seeking a specific bit of information, and he was probably in the majority, the classed catalogue did not serve too well. An extended search among the various classes and their numerous subdivisions was frequently necessary. Attempts were made to meet this difficulty by presenting the classification schedule in outline form at the beginning of the catalogue. William T. Harris felt that such a procedure made a complete understanding of the schedule unnecessary "for the scholar can run his eye over the four or five pages of subjects in the scheme in a few moments, even if he does not know the principles of classification."[11] Although the outline of the schedule was undoubtedly of assistance to the reader, it still did not enable him to find his subject easily and quickly.

The Classed Catalogue with an Alphabetical Index of Subjects

The middle of the nineteenth century finally saw an answer to the vexing problem of locating a particular subject in a complex classification schedule. This answer assumed the not surprising form of an alphabetical index of the subjects treated in the classed catalogue. The Philadelphia Mercantile Library Company appended to its 1850 classed catalogue "An Alphabetical List of Subjects."[12] In addition to the various classes and their subdivisions, the list

included "many topics whose position in the classified Catalogue
might not be indicated by the titles of the classes."[13] It also contained numerous entries for individual books. These references,
which took the form of subject-word entries, showed unmistakably
the influence of the alphabetical index of subjects which Jewett attached to his 1843 author catalogue of Brown University. The New
York Society Library also prepared a catalogue of its collections
in 1850 which had an "Alphabetical List of Subjects Contained in
the Analytical Catalogue."[14] This latter list, however, contained
few entries for specific works.

In the following years the small number of libraries that compiled alphabetical lists of the subjects treated in their classed catalogues attested, at least in part, to the difficulty of the task. Merely
to arrange the headings of the classes and subclasses in an alphabetical sequence was a simple procedure, and unfortunately one of
limited value; to extend the list to the point of true usefulness,
however, was far from a simple procedure, dependent as it was
upon the just emerging concept of subject headings. In 1876, Cutter
professed to know only three classed catalogues with alphabetical
lists of their subjects: those of the Philadelphia Mercantile Library Company in 1850, Newark Library Association in 1857, and
the California State Law Library in 1870.[15]

There were, however, a few others. The catalogue prepared
by the New York Society Library in 1850 has already been mentioned. The catalogue which S. Hastings Grant compiled for the
New York Mercantile Library in 1856 and the Peabody Institute
catalogue of 1861 were two more examples.[16] In its 1865 catalogue,
the New York Apprentices' Library included an alphabetical list of
over five hundred subjects which were in the classified index to the
main alphabetical sequence of entries.[17] The following year, 1866,
the Mercantile Library of the same city prepared an alphabetical
list of over twelve hundred subjects for a catalogue arranged in a
similar manner.[18] Even these more extensive lists, however, were
rather crude and incomplete. As late as 1876, Dewey wrote that he
was "aware that a subject index to accompany the classification
has been suggested," but that he had "...seen none that at all answers the purpose."[19] The ultimate classified catalogue with its
key—the alphabetical list of subjects—like the ultimate dictionary
catalogue was dependent upon, and would have to await, further development in the field of subject headings.

Criticisms of the Classed Catalogue

How was the classed catalogue regarded by the library leaders
of the day? For most of these men the answer is evident from an

examination of the catalogues they prepared and from their writings. Jewett, probably the outstanding librarian of the day, displayed an early and continuing dissatisfaction with the classed catalogue. Although some of his colleagues made prior and more vocal criticisms of logical classification, it was Jewett who first came forward with a practicable alternative. His rejection of a classified arrangement of subjects in favor of an alphabetical one in the Brown catalogue of 1843 has already been noted. Some ten years later, while engaged in formulating plans for stereotyping catalogues at the Smithsonian, Jewett again passed over a classified arrangement and advocated the alphabetical catalogue with an alphabetical index of subjects.[20] After becoming Superintendent of the Boston Public Library, Jewett compiled two of the outstanding catalogues of the day.[21] Upon both occasions he abandoned his former method of arrangement—not for a classed catalogue but, rather, for a dictionary. There is little evidence that Jewett ever had much enthusiasm for the classed catalogue.

William F. Poole found equally little of interest in the classed catalogue, for he, like Jewett, sought an alternative to logical classification. The dictionary arrangement which he introduced in the Boston Mercantile Library catalogue of 1854 provided a substitute for countless librarians dissatisfied with the classified arrangement. Poole's opinions on the proper arrangement of catalogues remained unchanged through the years. In 1870 he supervised the compilation of a dictionary catalogue for the Silas Bronson Library of Waterbury, Connecticut.[22] The following year he prepared a dictionary catalogue for the Cincinnati Public Library.[23] In 1876 he wrote that "the plan of catalogue with references under the authors and subjects, in one alphabetical arrangement, is the one which is now almost universally used, and is preferable to the classified plan."[24]

Ezra Abbot, in his earlier years at least, did not share Jewett's and Poole's dissatisfaction with the classed catalogue. In 1853, while Librarian of the Cambridge, Massachusetts, High School, Abbot compiled a closely classed catalogue of the library with an alphabetical index of authors and titles.[25] The ensuing ten years, however, saw a decided change in his views on the proper arrangement of catalogues. In 1861, as Superintendent of the Catalogue Department of Harvard College Library, he devised an alphabetico-classed arrangement for that institution's new subject catalogue on cards. In a report to an Examining Committee of the Overseers of Harvard College, Abbot disclosed his reasons for not adopting a purely classified arrangement. The classed catalogue without minute subdivisions has the "great objection" of "excessive generality," he wrote;[26] with minute subdivisions it has the difficulty that "before an uninitiated person can ascertain in what part of the arrangement he is to look for his subject, he must make himself master of a very complex system of classification."[27]

Joseph Green Cogswell, like Abbot, initially appeared to favor the classified arrangement for catalogues. In one of his early reports as Superintendent of the Astor Library, Cogswell expressed to the Trustees his desire to prepare a broadly classed catalogue of the collections, to be printed a section at a time as each department was completed.[28] When the catalogue appeared a few years later, however, it assumed quite a different form. The first portion to be published was an alphabetical catalogue of author and anonymous title entries.[29] In the preface Cogswell announced the Astor's intention to print an alphabetical index of subjects in the near future—a scheme with which he was obviously in accord, for he stated that it was "the only unobjectionable plan...[and] the one which renders the library most easy of consultation."[30]

Among the library leaders of the day Cutter was very possibly the best informed concerning the merits of the various methods of catalogue arrangement, and he was certainly not unaware of the peculiar benefits of logical classification. Despite the unique advantages of the classed catalogue, Cutter felt that "the necessity of mastering a complex system before using the catalogue is an unwelcome delay or an absolute bar to its use."[31] He acknowledged, however, that there was a simple and obvious remedy—an alphabetical list of subjects—which would "almost remove all these difficulties."[32] Nevertheless, although he was later to publish his *Expansive Classification,*[33] during the period under review Cutter was almost the personification of the dictionary catalogue. Both the catalogue he prepared for the Boston Athenaeum in 1874-82, and its by-product, the *Rules for a Printed Dictionary Catalogue,*[34] were regarded as milestones at the time, and their significance has paled little with the passage of years.

Although Melvil Dewey was not born at the beginning of this period, by its end twenty-five years later he was the acknowledged champion of the classified arrangement. "No one questions," he stated categorically in 1876, "the immense superiority of a satisfactory classed catalogue."[35] Even Dewey recognized, however, that the great difficulty of making and using the classed catalogue had caused many librarians to abandon it as impracticable. Like the majority of his colleagues, he was also aware that an alphabetical list of the subjects included in the classed catalogue would solve most of the problems; but, unlike his colleagues, he was able to devise this alphabetical list—and therein lay his genius. His "Relativ Index,"[36] as he termed it, henceforth made possible the compilation of highly effective classed catalogues. But Dewey's idea did not come until the end of this period, a period which was clearly dominated by another type of catalogue—the dictionary.

THE DICTIONARY ARRANGEMENT

By 1875 the modern dictionary catalogue had been conceived in its essentials—at least in the mind of Cutter. With the publication of the first volume of the great dictionary catalogue of the Boston Athenaeum in 1874, Cutter had even given his ideas substantive form. By his own admission, however, Cutter was in many ways dissatisfied with this monumental work,[37] and it was in his *Rules for a Printed Dictionary Catalogue* that his ideas were most fully developed.

What sort of a catalogue did Cutter envision? The greater number of his *Rules for a Printed Dictionary Catalogue* were equally applicable to any of several forms of catalogues; however, as their title indicated, they were primarily intended for a printed dictionary catalogue. In Cutter's mind the dictionary catalogue consisted of an author catalogue, more or less complete title and form catalogues, and an alphabetical subject catalogue employing true subject entries—all interfiled in one alphabetical sequence and tied together with a carefully constructed network of cross references. Such a sophisticated catalogue obviously was long in evolution. Although Cutter's contributions toward it were notable—perhaps even critical—they were quite dependent upon the previous efforts of several librarians, especially Jewett, Abbot, and Poole.

During its formative period, particularly, the dictionary catalogue meant widely different things to different librarians. Essential to virtually everyone's conception of the dictionary catalogue, however, were two features. The first was the interfiling of different types of entries, i.e., author entries, title entries, subject entries, and so on, in one alphabetical sequence rather than in several separate and distinct sequences, as was customarily done. The other feature was the practice of presenting the subjects of books by the use of specific subject entries rather than by the traditional class entries. A work was entered directly under a heading which was intended to express the precise subject of the book, not under a class which included that subject. The resulting subject entries were then arranged alphabetically in the same sequence with whatever author and title entries were at hand. Probably the first catalogue in America to incorporate both of these features was that which Poole prepared for the Boston Mercantile Library in 1854. But before Poole's catalogue is examined in detail, the origins of those features which made his work possible should be traced.

Origins of the Dictionary Arrangement

In library catalogues the practice of interfiling author and title entries in a single alphabetical arrangement is quite as old as the alphabetical arrangement itself. Every collection of books, however small, had its share of anonymous works which were entered under some word in the title, usually the leading or most prominent word. Although upon occasion, as in the 1807 catalogue of the Library Company of Philadelphia, these anonymous title entries were placed in a separate sequence, the usual practice was to interfile them with the author entries. As librarians sought to make their catalogues more useful for locating books, they began to enter books with personal authors under both the author and the title, especially if the title contained a significant word by which it might be remembered. Cutter noted that between 1815 and 1854 there were nineteen catalogues so prepared, with the percentage of title entries increasing markedly.[38] The practice reached its height in the 1844 catalogue of the Boston Mercantile Library which, as a matter of course, entered all books under both their authors and their titles, whenever practicable.[39]

Interfiling subject entries alphabetically with author and title entries was a comparatively late development and impossible so long as the subject entries were logically classed. The appearance of Jewett's alphabetically arranged subject index in the 1843 Brown University catalogue, however, removed this last obstacle to the interfiling in a single alphabetical sequence of author, title, and subject entries.

The second feature necessary for the dictionary catalogue, it will be recalled, was the use of specific subject entries. This innovation was introduced into American library catalogues by Jewett in the form of an alphabetical subject index appended to the Brown University author catalogue of 1843. Only infrequently did the subject entries in Jewett's index go beyond the wording of the title. In this form, of course, they approximated the title entries of the day, and one may reasonably inquire what advance Jewett made. His contribution was this: although he did not see fit to carry through with it himself, Jewett had devised a system of subject entries which permitted their being interfiled alphabetically with author and title entries. Thus, by the middle of the nineteenth century, the essential elements of the dictionary catalogue were in existence and needed only to be joined by an imaginative and resourceful librarian.

Poole's Dictionary Catalogue of the Boston Mercantile Library

It was not necessary to wait many years before such a librarian appeared—William F. Poole. The catalogue which he prepared for the Boston Mercantile Library in 1854, although incompletely conceived and incompletely carried out, is clearly recognizable as the forerunner of the modern dictionary catalogue. That Poole should have introduced the dictionary arrangement into American library catalogues was by no means chance. He had employed a similar arrangement in his *Index to Periodical Literature*, which by 1853 had already appeared in two editions.[40] He drew heavily from this experience in preparing the Boston Mercantile Library catalogue, the plan of which he described thus:

> The plan of the work will be best understood by an examination of the Catalogue itself. It will be seen that short titles have been adopted; that each work has been catalogued under its author and under its subject, and works of fiction have been placed under their titles as well as authors. The whole being arranged in one alphabetical series, a work can be easily found, if either its author, subject, or title is known.[41]

For all entries Poole included the place and date of publication, size, number of volumes if more than one, and the book location number; nevertheless, by the use of brief titles and frequent abbreviations, he was able to confine the entry to a single line of type in most instances. The catalogue contained no cross references, no contents notes, and no entries for parts of books.

Poole's catalogue gave evidence of shrewd and careful planning. Even readers having slight familiarity with libraries found it easy to use, for its alphabetical and dictionary-type arrangement was readily understood. The subject-word entries, despite their many shortcomings, furnished a fair indication of the contents of most of the books. And fortunately the preceding advantages were gained in a catalogue which was remarkably simple to compile. Brief entries were made for each book under the author and under that word of the title most suggestive of the content. In the case of fictional works, an entry under the first word of the title was substituted for the subject-word entry. Avoided were the many time-consuming problems attending the preparation of a minutely classed catalogue. The omission of all cross references, entries for parts of books, and notes listing the contents of books also expedited the labor of compilation. Finally, through the use of brief title entries and other economies, the catalogue could be printed at a minimum cost.

Despite its ease of compilation and economy of printing, Poole' catalogue was surprisingly useful and was enthusiastically received by librarians of the day. The following year, 1855, it served as a model for the catalogue which the Cincinnati Young Men's Mercantile Library prepared for its collections. In the years that followed, other libraries adopted its plan outright for their catalogues, and still more libraries used it with modifications.

Popular as was Poole's catalogue, it was only the first step in the development of the modern dictionary catalogue, and it exhibited several shortcomings which were immediately apparent. Perhaps most serious was its use of subject-word entries. To be limited in the selection of a subject entry to the wording used by the author in his title produced several complications. Works on precisely the same subject, for example, were separated in the catalogue if their authors chanced to use only synonymous terms rather than identical terms in the titles. Conversely, works on quite different subjects were brought together and interfiled if the subject word selected for their entry had multiple meanings. Another objection, frequently connected with but not peculiar to the use of subject-word entries, was Poole's failure to enter polytopical works under more than a single subject.

Some of the faults of Poole's subject-word entries could have been minimized had he used cross references—and therein lay another serious defect in his catalogue. Although the users of his catalogue would still not have found all of the titles on a particular subject in a single place, they would at least have been referred to those other places where additional material was to be found. As it was, readers were at the mercy of their imaginations in thinking of all the various words under which material on a given subject might be located.

Although Poole firmly believed that his plan of catalogue provided the reader with a subject approach, the evidence suggests that he had a limited appreciation of what was involved. Rather than preparing a tool to inform the reader of all the books in the library on various subjects, Poole appears to have had in mind the providing of still another means for locating books with which the reader was already familiar—a subject approach which could be employed in the event that either the author or the title of the book was forgotten. To repeat a portion of his own statement of the plan of his catalogue, "a work can be easily found, if either its author, *subject* [underlining mine], or title is known."[42] His failure to connect synonymous subject headings by using cross references can be cited as further evidence for this contention. Finally, the entries under a subject word were arranged alphabetically by the first word of that portion of the title following the subject word. Had Poole's primary concern been to reveal which authors had written upon a particular subject, the subarrangement would logically have been by author.

Considering Poole's long experience in indexing periodicals, he was undoubtedly aware of the disadvantages to the plan which he selected for his first library catalogue; and his retention of the same general plan in later catalogues could only have been done with a full understanding of the results. The catalogue which Fletcher prepared under Poole's direction in 1870 for the Silas Bronson Library in Waterbury, Connecticut, differed in no essential from Poole's original plan. Neither did the catalogue which Poole himself prepared a year later for the Cincinnati Public Library.

In his discussion of plans for the third edition of his *Index to Periodical Literature,* Poole made his views concerning the use of cross references unmistakably clear:

> ...Nor do I expect by cross-references to relieve the reader from using the best quality of brain he possesses. In most instances, persons who use such an index have intelligence enough to know, without being told, the subjects which are nearly related to the one in which they are interested. If every subject shall have cross-references to its allies, the work will be mainly a book of cross-references, rather than an index to subjects. [43]

Upon reflection, Poole's views concerning the proper methods of catalogue compilation were not at the time, and are not now, wholly untenable. He was simply of the opinion that only so much time and effort could profitably be devoted to the compilation of a catalogue, and that within these limits no plan was superior to his own. In Poole's defense it should be noted that he prepared useful catalogues for the Boston Mercantile Library within two years of his arrival, for the Cincinnati Public Library the year he arrived, and for the Chicago Public Library the year after.[44] With the Boston Athenaeum, however, he was not so successful. Upon his departure from that institution in 1869, its catalogue was no nearer completion than when he had arrived thirteen years earlier.[45]

The objections to Poole's methods, which have perhaps been treated too fully, should not be allowed to obscure his great contribution to the development of the dictionary catalogue. In America it was he who first laid out the plan and constructed a workable catalogue upon it.

Jewett's Catalogues of the Boston Public Library

Improvements upon Poole's dictionary catalogue were

forthcoming shortly and from a not unexpected source—Jewett. Although Poole could claim priority in the introduction of the dictionary arrangement, in most aspects of catalogue preparation he had
much to learn from Jewett. This was particularly true of the subject portion of the catalogue. More than ten years before the appearance of Poole's dictionary catalogue, Jewett had, of course, appended to the 1843 author catalogue of Brown University an alphabetical subject index. This index was better prepared and exhibited
a considerably fuller understanding of the subject approach than
did the subject portion of Poole's dictionary catalogue. For example, Jewett employed cross references freely and effectively. He
also arranged the entries under the various subject headings alphabetically by author—a procedure that assisted those readers in
search of books upon a particular subject. Poole, it will be recalled, let the wording of the title dictate the order of arrangement,
a practice which favored those readers who might use subject entries to locate books already known to them.

Jewett retained his preference for the author catalogue with a
separate alphabetical index of subjects until at least 1853 when his
report ... *On the Construction of Catalogues* ... appeared. Although
this publication was primarily concerned with plans for printing a
general catalogue of the holdings of American libraries, Jewett
took the occasion to express his views concerning the type of catalogue which individual libraries should prepare for their collections:

> ... Alphabetical catalogues are to be preferred. ... Such
> is now the general opinion of competent bibliographers and
> literary men.
> . . . .
> In connection with the catalogue of each library, there should
> be an index of subjects. This index should also be alphabet-
> ical.[46]

The appearance of Poole's catalogue in 1854, with all of its entries
interfiled in a single alphabetical sequence, must have altered
Jewett's thinking considerably; the catalogues he prepared after
assuming his duties at the Boston Public Library in 1855 employed
a similar arrangement.

It was a dispirited Jewett—loser in his struggle with Joseph
Henry, secretary of the Smithsonian Institution, to make of the
Smithsonian a national library—who arrived at the Boston Public
Library in 1855 to assist in the preparation of their catalogues.
He threw himself into his work, and shortly was deeply engaged in
the preparation of a catalogue on cards which gave "the title of
every book fully, and it is hoped with accuracy, together with very
numerous cross-references from the subjects of the books and the

words of the titles."[47] Jewett hoped to print a full and accurate
catalogue of the entire collection at the earliest possible date.
George Ticknor, founder of the Boston Public Library, intervened,
however, with the suggestion that a catalogue should first be
printed of the popular, circulating collection in the Lower Hall.
Whatever may have been Jewett's personal preference, he immediately set about carrying out Ticknor's wishes, and the catalogue
appeared in 1858. In its preface Jewett was careful to point out
that the word "Index" had been used advisedly in the title, for the
work was but an abridgment of the complete catalogue which was
on cards.[48]

Jewett's intention was to provide a catalogue "which will be
exact and simple, requiring no elaborate explanation of its plan or
of the way to use it."[49] He described his plan thus:

> It contains a brief title of every work, under the name of
> the author, with a designation of the place, and date of publi-
> cation, and of the size of the book. Each book is entered again
> under the word denoting its subject, and yet again under any
> prominent word in its title under which it would be likely to be
> sought for. These names of authors, of titles, and of subjects,
> are arranged in one alphabetical series, so that the work can
> be consulted with the greatest facility. It is difficult to see
> how anything of the kind can be simpler.[50]

To complete the description of Jewett's catalogue, it should be
added that cross references were liberally and intelligently used;
the contents of multiwork volumes were listed in detail; bibliographical notes accompanied many of the titles; and bibliographical
essays were prepared on numerous subjects. There were, however, no subject entries for works occupying less than a physical
volume. There were also no entries for individual articles in periodicals or for separate papers in the proceedings and transactions
of learned societies. A work was entered under the name of its
author whenever it could be ascertained; anonymous works were
entered under the first word of the title which was not an article.
Lastly, accompanying each entry was a book location number.

Those respects in which Jewett's catalogue represented an
advance over that of Poole's were several and, as Poole would undoubtedly have pointed out, not obtained without the expenditure of
much time and money. Fundamental to Poole's thinking was the
idea that the search for information for cataloguing a book should
not extend beyond the covers of the book itself. Not so with Jewett,
who displayed a definite concern for uncovering the identity of the
authors of works published anonymously or pseudonymously. He
also exhibited great care in distinguishing authors' names—

particularly those apt to be confused—by the use of birth and death dates and by appending brief biographical phrases. For those works which might be catalogued under different headings and, more importantly, sought for under different headings, Jewett was careful to prepare all the necessary cross references to the entry selected.

The greatest improvement was Jewett's use of cross references. One of the major drawbacks of even the best dictionary catalogue was the dispersal of related materials throughout the entire alphabetical sequence. The use of subject-word headings rather than true subject headings compounded this disadvantage, since material on the same subject was dispersed according to the terminology which the authors chanced to employ in their titles. Under these conditions the importance of a finely executed system of cross references was undeniable.

Jewett's subject entries were a substantial improvement over previous efforts and, at the same time, a major defect of his catalogue. Although there were many instances of the use of subject headings in the modern sense, the catalogue still contained numerous synonymous headings and awkwardly phrased catch-title entries. Jewett did, however, make multiple entries for polytopical works. Of especial significance was his decision to list the various entries on a subject alphabetically by author rather than by title. This enabled librarians for the first time to distinguish between subject and title entries and to arrive at the proper function of each.

Another unfortunate aspect of Jewett's catalogue was his method of handling the subject approach. Instead of full added entries, Jewett employed only brief author-title references. For information concerning the imprint and other particulars of the book, the reader was expected to turn to the full entry under the author. This was a policy which even Poole, in all his haste and concern with economy, did not adopt. Jewett was only continuing a practice he had instituted earlier in the Brown catalogue. This procedure eventually earned for Jewett the censure of several of his colleagues, and of Ezra Abbot in particular, who stated the case thus:

> The wants of a person who is seeking information on a particular subject are not met by a huge collection of references, which leave him in the dark as to the size, date, edition, number of volumes, and place of publication of the works referred to, and merely send him to different parts of the alphabet of a long catalogue; he needs before him, for examination and comparison, the full titles of the volumes to which reference is made, so far as they relate to the subject in question.[51]

In spite of considerable criticism Jewett's method of subject cross references gained many adherents in the following years.

Jewett's catalogue of the books in the Bates Collection in the Upper Hall of the Boston Public Library appeared in 1861. Although better executed and somewhat fuller in bibliographical detail, this second catalogue was prepared according to the same general plan as the first.

The appearance of Jewett's catalogues of the Boston Public Library brought forth an unparalleled flood of congratulatory letters and journal articles. In his biography of Jewett, Joseph A. Borome refers at length to the highly favorable comments received from the noted London bookseller and bibliographer Henry Stevens, Daniel Coit Gilman of Yale University, President Felton of Harvard, and from librarians Justin Winsor, Lloyd P. Smith, Samuel Foster Haven, and Joseph Green Cogswell.[52] Probably most satisfying to Jewett were the many catalogues prepared according to his plan, the most notable of which were those of the Philadelphia Mercantile Library in 1870 and the Buffalo Young Men's Association Library in 1871.[53]

Abbot's Alphabetico-classed Catalogue

A few months after the completion of Jewett's second catalogue of the Boston Public Library, Ezra Abbot, Superintendent of the Cataloguing Department of the Harvard University Library, began to prepare a catalogue on cards for the use of students and faculty in Cambridge. Although this catalogue was never published, it exerted a marked influence upon the printed catalogues of the day. Abbot's plan was to prepare two separate catalogues, one of which he termed an "Index of Authors," the other an "Index of Subjects."[54] Although both were well planned and skillfully executed, the latter catalogue represented the advance in cataloguing practice and attracted the more attention. Fundamental to its plan was the idea that each book should have a subject entry—more than one if necessary—which would be determined solely by its content and not, in Abbot's words, "merely by the accidental phraseology of the title."[55] Although for some time entries taken from the title had been giving way to subject entries, Abbot's statement marked the first instance in which the provision of true subject headings was made a matter of conscious and announced policy.

For the arrangement of his "Index of Subjects," Abbot was dissatisfied with all three of the practices then current. An unfortunate prerequisite for the use of the closely classed catalogue, he noted, was the mastery of a complex classification schedule; the broadly classed catalogue he condemned for its "excessive

generality."[56] He acknowledged a certain personal attraction to the
dictionary catalogue, at least in comparison with either of the preceding two systems. In its present form, however, he was much
distressed by one particular defect it possessed—that of "tearing
violently asunder and scattering through the whole alphabet those
subjects which nature has joined together."[57] Through the correction of this fault Abbot arrived at his method of arrangement, which
he described thus:

> In this plan, the arrangement of classes or subjects is
> *alphabetical*, not *scientific;* but it differs from the scheme just
> remarked upon ₍the dictionary arrangement₎ in this, that a
> large part of these classes or subjects have numerous *subdi-*
> *visions*, which, instead of being dispersed through the great
> alphabetical series, and thus widely separated from each other,
> are arranged in a *secondary alphabetical series under the gen-*
> *eral head.*[58]

The plan, of course, is immediately recognized as the "alphabetico-
classed system" or the "mixed system;" indeed, Cutter so defined
it as early as 1869.[59]

Despite Abbot's protests to the contrary the alphabetico-
classed system, like each of the other systems, had its flaw. The
constant question was whether a particular subject should be treated
independently and placed in the main alphabetical sequence, or subordinated to a larger subject of which it might be considered a part.
Although in either event proper cross references led the user to
his desired subject, there was the possibility that he would be put
to an extra step. It is to Abbot's credit that he was aware of this
problem from the beginning; he believed, however, that in most instances the proper choice was made quite apparent by the surrounding circumstances.[60] How correct was Abbot in this contention?

Two distinguished librarians of the day—Charles A. Cutter and
Justin Winsor—had occasion to observe Abbot's work closely. Cutter served as Abbot's assistant during much of the formative period
of the catalogue, and Winsor, as a practicing scholar and as Harvard
librarian, was in a unique position to judge the effectiveness of the
catalogue. Although Cutter's enthusiasm may have waned slightly
with the years, he had a high regard for the alphabetico-classed
catalogue—at least as it was worked out by Abbot. Upon going to
the Boston Athenaeum as librarian in 1868, Cutter confessed to a
preference for the alphabetico-classed plan and a reluctance to
begin the great dictionary catalogue he was to compile for that library.[61] A year later his highly favorable article on "The New Catalogue of Harvard College Library" appeared in the *North American*
Review.[62]

By 1876, however, Cutter was willing to concede that between the dictionary and the alphabetico-classed systems "there is very little difference in their convenience for a person who understands both. The Abbot system is best adapted for the thorough investigation of comprehensive subjects; the dictionary system for finding quickly what relates to a person, a place, or other special topic."[63]

Winsor's experience in using the Harvard alphabetico-classed catalogue did not permit him to agree with Cutter. Winsor noted simply and bluntly that "a classified system, or the mongrel alphabetico-classed system, as it is called, is practically a nuisance, and I have daily consciousness of it."[64]

Winsor's reactions were typical of those of librarians and readers in general, for the alphabetico-classed system never attained much popularity in the libraries of the United States. An occasional catalogue was thus prepared, the most notable of which was that of the Library of Congress in 1869. This work, which appeared in two volumes, was appropriately termed an *Index of Subjects,* and was prepared according to the plan of Abbot, with modifications. In some instances the arrangement of the parts of a subject under that subject was other than alphabetical. The names of places, for example, were not subordinated either to the class "Geography" or to other broad geographical terms; rather, they were treated independently and entered directly in the main alphabetical sequence. In the majority of cases the subject headings were based upon the contents of the books and not upon merely the wording of their titles. A finely executed system of cross references was set up between related subjects, and from specific subjects to those general subjects of which they were a part.

Schwartz's Combined Dictionary-classed Catalogue

Another librarian who was dissatisfied with both the classified and the dictionary arrangements was Jacob Schwartz of the New York Apprentices' Library. Like Abbot, Schwartz desired to secure in some way the benefits of both systems; unlike Abbot, who sought to merge the two into a single plan—the alphabetico-classed —Schwartz was convinced that the plans "cannot be united without doing violence to the principles upon which each is based."[65] His solution was to consider them as equally important parts of the whole; for, he noted, "each is admirable in its way—the one for general information concerning classes, and the other for specific information concerning individuals."

Specifically, the plan which Schwartz employed consisted of three parts. Each work was initially entered briefly and without imprint in a classified sequence. Following this was an alphabetical

sequence of catch-title and subject-word entries, again brief and
without imprint. The final sequence was a catalogue of full author
entries. Such a catalogue, Schwartz declared, "answers all the
possible and legitimate inquiries that can be directed to a catalogue, whether general or specific, in the shortest and most direct
manner." [66]

The objections to Schwartz's plan are so apparent as scarcely
to require noting. His catalogue was, in reality, two catalogues;
and the cost of its preparation was also that of two catalogues.
The subject entries in the alphabetical portion of the catalogue
lacked fullness and carried no imprints. The same was true of the
entries in the classed portion. The result was that constant reference was necessary to the author catalogue for details concerning
full title, edition, date and place of publication, and the like. In the
plan of his catalogue Schwartz had quite clearly introduced no startling innovations that were likely to be embraced by other libraries.

Cutter's Dictionary Catalogue of the Boston Athenaeum

The appearance in 1874 of the first volume of the monumental
catalogue of the Boston Athenaeum represented a double victory.
It was, naturally, a great personal triumph for Cutter and striking
evidence of his cataloguing genius; it was also a triumph for American librarianship. Cutter's work was based squarely upon that of
Oliver A. Taylor, Jewett, Poole, Abbot, and others, and represented,
in a sense, the culmination of their efforts.

The Boston Athenaeum catalogue was neither quickly nor easily
produced. Work upon it began in 1856, the year in which Poole was
appointed librarian. At that time the decision was made to print a
catalogue similar in plan to the one Poole had completed two years
before for the Boston Mercantile Library. Poole entrusted its
preparation to several young men with no previous cataloguing experience and who, unfortunately, were left to their own devices.
By 1862 it was apparent to Poole that little progress was being
made, whereupon he placed Charles R. Lowell, brother of the poet,
in full charge. After a period of trial and error Lowell, who was
of a meticulous and scholarly mind, began to do creditable work.
Suddenly, in 1870, Lowell died in the midst of his labors, and the
responsibility for the catalogue fell to Cutter, who had replaced
Poole as librarian one year before.

Cutter's was not an enviable inheritance. The work passed on
to him was in poor repair, and the Trustees, wearied with waiting
for a catalogue, were clamoring for immediate publication. Cutter's task was rendered even more formidable by his own high
standards of workmanship and impatience with anything less.

However discouraging the situation may have been for Cutter, he immediately began work. As he examined the cataloguing of his predecessors, he must have been sorely tempted to start anew, for he found little that he could accept.

Especially unsatisfactory to Cutter were many of the incomplete and hastily conceived entries—a situation which he felt compelled to correct. Intensive efforts were made to establish the full names of all authors and to distinguish between those with the same names. Exhaustive searches were also made to uncover the authors of works published anonymously or pseudonymously, with works being entered under their true authors when found. Those anonymously published works for which authors were not found were then systematically entered under the first word of the title which was not an article or a preposition. Confusion also existed in the entering of corporate publications—a difficulty which Cutter was able to reduce but by no means dispel.

Bibliographical description was little better. The titles had been carelessly and inaccurately copied and, in many instances, abridged beyond recognition. The edition of the work was seldom noted. Omitted frequently were the imprints, especially for the subject entries. Cutter corrected all of these defects and others, too.

Completely unacceptable to Cutter was the work which had been done on the subject entries and on the supporting system of cross references. Although subject entries had been prepared for most of the books, they were made according to Poole's plan, i.e., they were catchword entries drawn from the terminology of the titles. For these entries Cutter substituted true subject entries—more than 6,000 of them—which were based solely on the content of the books. Little progress had been made on the task of connecting the thousands of subject entries with cross references. Cutter, who considered this feature to be an integral part of the dictionary catalogue, systematically made cross references between coordinate subjects and from general subjects to subordinate subjects. Their use, he believed, minimized the ill effects of dispersing material on related subjects throughout the alphabet and regained some of the values of the classified arrangement.

Cutter had long been disturbed by the amount of excellent material in libraries that went undetected, and thus unused, because of the failure of cataloguing practices to describe works occupying but a part of a physical volume. Accordingly, he methodically included under the main entry lists of the contents of those books which contained several works by the same or by different authors. He also prepared separate analytical entries for many of these parts of books under their authors, subjects, and titles. Individual articles in many periodicals and society publications were similarly treated.

Finally, after Cutter assumed direction of the catalogue, the number of volumes included was increased by one third. Even so, no work added to the collections after 1871 appeared in the catalogue.

Cutter's catalogue was immediately recognized as an outstanding piece of work and for many years represented the culmination of the art of catalogue making. Even today, almost a century later, librarians have not ceased to be amazed by its order, its accuracy, and its completeness.

The enthusiastic reception accorded Cutter's catalogue assured the predominance of the dictionary arrangement in American library catalogues for years to come. Although the perspective of time has clarified the respective merits of the classified and the dictionary arrangements, it has not enabled most observers to state categorically which is better. The classed catalogue had the invaluable facility of grouping related materials together in meaningful order. Such an arrangement, of course, accommodated the reader interested in the intensive and protracted study of a subject. An unfortunate prerequisite for the efficient use of the classed catalogue was the necessity of either first learning the classification system or referring to an outline of the scheme before searching for a subject. This disadvantage was emphasized by the existence of numerous classification systems during this period. Although the difficulty was in part removed by the preparation of alphabetical indexes of the subjects treated in the classification schedules, it could never be entirely avoided.

The great—and unique—value of the dictionary catalogue was that it could be used immediately and easily by anyone familiar with the alphabet; however, considerably more than a mere knowledge of the alphabet was required if maximum benefits were to be extracted from the catalogue. The serious weakness of the dictionary arrangement lay, of course, in its dispersal of related materials throughout the alphabetical sequence—a defect not entirely remedied by even the best system of cross references. In summary, both arrangements had their particular merits and were not really in competition in the sense of performing the same task; they were, however, in competition in the sense that libraries were forced to choose between them.

Chapter V

The Decline of the Printed Book Catalogue

The final quarter of the nineteenth century witnessed the passing of the printed book catalogue as the medium for listing library collections. This was in large part accomplished by the same two forces that had undermined the book catalogue in the preceding quarter century: the spectacular and unrelenting growth of library collections and the expanding function of the catalogue.[1]

Although the dramatic growth of American libraries during the latter part of the last century has been described many times, it is repeated briefly here because of its significance for the book catalogue. In 1876 the largest library in the country, the Library of Congress, could claim no more than 300,000 volumes; by 1900, the collections of five more libraries had reached that figure, and the Library of Congress had become America's first 1,000,000-volume library. Nor was this spectacular growth limited to a few of the larger libraries. In 1876 only ten libraries had 100,000 volumes; in 1900 no fewer than fifty-two had reached that figure. In this same interval of time the Chicago Public Library had increased its collections fivefold; the New York State Library, fourfold; the Library of Congress and the Cincinnati Public, threefold; and Yale, Harvard, and the Boston Public Library had each doubled.

At the beginning of this period the University of Chicago, Enoch Pratt, and Newberry libraries were not even in existence; by 1900, however, they had joined the front ranks of American libraries. Even the hard-pressed society libraries recorded remarkable growths. The St. Louis Mercantile Library, the Boston Athenaeum, and the Library Company of Philadelphia, for example, each doubled in size. Such tremendous growths struck the printed book catalogue at its most vulnerable point—the difficulty of keeping pace with swelling book collections.[1]

76

The second force—the broadened objectives which libraries were assuming, with the attendant implications for library catalogues—also may be stressed here. In 1875 the primary function of the library was still regarded in most quarters to be the acquisition and preservation of books. To serve this limited purpose a fairly simple catalogue sufficed. Rapidly gaining acceptance, however, was the idea that the library should also make the books readily available to all qualified users. Readers were not only to be supplied with specific books they might request on a subject, but also to be informed of the library's other holdings in the area. By 1900 this concept was generally accepted by American librarians, and its consequences for catalogues were only too well known. More than a generation of cataloguers had struggled, in what at times must have seemed to be a vain effort, to lay out for a multitude of readers the complete subject resources of their libraries.

But the end was not yet. William I. Fletcher and others were espousing the aggressive view that the public library was nothing less than "an agency established in the name of the community to accomplish definite results in public culture through the use of books."[2] Inconsistent with such a high purpose, they maintained, was the libraries' practice of issuing bare lists of their books, leaving the reader to an uninstructed choice among them. Only by evaluating the worth of these books and by fostering the reading of the best, they argued, could the library properly discharge its responsibilities. The "annotated" or "educational" catalogues were the result.

The above considerations so increased the expense of printing catalogues that the majority of libraries were compelled, even before 1875, to abandon the printed book catalogue or seriously to curtail its fullness. A few libraries, however, continued to print until the coming of the Library of Congress printed cards in 1901, and an occasional library even printed beyond that date. In his *Public Libraries in America,* first published in 1894, Fletcher observed matter-of-factly that "printed catalogues of public libraries have nearly had their day."[3] Significantly, he also noted that the card catalogue "is now so nearly universal [in America] that it may almost be said to be the only method in general use."[4] Neither statement was challenged in the reviews of the day, nor were there grounds for challenge.

In 1885 the librarian of the St. Louis Public Library, Frederick M. Crunden, polled his colleagues concerning the form of catalogue in use in their libraries.[5] Of the 108 librarians responding to his questionnaire, 25 reported that they depended chiefly or entirely on printed catalogues; 36 reported card catalogues only; and 47 indicated they used both printed and card catalogues. The majority of the libraries in the final category were using card catalogues to supplement book catalogues printed some years previously and probably had little intention of further printing.

A decade later William C. Lane, librarian of Harvard University, made a similar inquiry for a paper he presented at the World's Library Congress in Chicago.[6] Reporting on the cataloguing practices of "each of 58 representative and well-known libraries,"[7] Lane noted that only the Peabody Institute in Baltimore had an up-to-date printed catalogue and that only thirteen libraries had book catalogues kept current with card supplements. All of the remaining libraries depended upon complete or nearly complete card catalogues; however, it should be noted that several of these libraries printed bulletins of their recent acquisitions and finding lists for the most used portions of their collections.

In 1900, of the fifty-two libraries in the United States with more than 100,000 volumes, only three had published full catalogues in the preceding decade: Peabody Institute in Baltimore, the Carnegie Library in Pittsburgh, and the Surgeon-General's Office in Washington, D.C.[8] In the previous quarter century, only one third of these same libraries had succeeded in printing full catalogues of their collections. Of the remaining two thirds, only about one half had printed even finding lists of substantial portions of their books.

A final and conclusive blow to the printed book catalogue was struck by the Library of Congress at the end of the century. Its admirable scheme for the production and distribution of catalogue cards placed an excellent printed catalogue on cards within the reach of even the humblest library, and rendered the printed book catalogue a luxury that even the richest library could ill afford.

THE MONUMENTAL DICTIONARY CATALOGUES

During the latter years of the nineteenth century the printed book catalogue, while drawing its final breath, experienced its finest hour. Paradoxical as this may appear, it can readily be understood that the expense of producing these excellent catalogues precipitated their end, as nothing else could have done, by demonstrating the impossibility of maintaining full and up-to-date printed book catalogues of rapidly expanding collections.

The pioneer among these monumental catalogues was prepared by Cutter for the collections of the Boston Athenaeum. The first of the five volumes comprising this catalogue was published in 1874, the last in 1882. In 1880, two years before the completion of the Boston Athenaeum catalogue, the first volume of the *Index-Catalogue of the Library of the Surgeon-General's Office* appeared.[9] Fifteen years elapsed before Dr. John Shaw Billings brought out the six-

teenth and final volume of the first series of this magnificent catalogue. Although Dr. Billings resigned in 1895 to become the first
librarian of the Public Library in New York City, the catalogue he
had started was continued in much the same form until 1948. [10] In
1883 the great catalogues of the Boston Athenaeum and the Surgeon-
General's Office were joined by a third—the *Catalogue of the Library of the Peabody Institute.*[11] This catalogue, which was completed in five volumes in 1892, was followed by the *Second Catalogue of the Library of the Peabody Institute,*[12] an even fuller and
more comprehensive work which was published in eight volumes
between the years 1896 and 1905.

To what do the great catalogues of the Boston Athenaeum, the
Peabody Institute, and the Surgeon-General's Office owe their distinction? They were, first of all, catalogues of large and scholarly
collections. The three libraries each contained about 100,000
books, plus undetermined numbers of pamphlets. But catalogues
of equally large and scholarly collections had been prepared before
without attracting undue note. There was, for example, Joseph
Green Cogswell's catalogue of the Astor Library, printed in the
years 1857-61, and seven years later the alphabetico-classed catalogue of the Library of Congress. Both collections numbered in
excess of 100,000 volumes. Clearly, the indexing of a large and
well-selected library did not alone ensure an outstanding catalogue.

In plan, all three catalogues were carefully conceived and ex-
pertly carried out. In the Boston Athenaeum catalogue Cutter produced what has generally been regarded as the finest example of
the dictionary scheme and of cataloguing technique. His entries—
prepared for author, title, and subject—were fully and accurately
made and were skillfully tied together with a network of cross references. The other two catalogues were similar in plan to Cutter's
and followed it in point of time; however, their compilers were
willing to acknowledge something less than full indebtedness to
him. In the preface to the *Index-Catalogue,* Dr. Billings stated that
the plan of the work was that preferred by the majority of the
American medical profession.[13] Although the first volume of the
Peabody catalogue was not published until 1883, work on it had begun in 1869. At that time, as the editor later pointed out, "Mr.
Cutter's excellent rules ... had not appeared; and the first volume
of his able catalogue of the Athenaeum Library was not published
till 1874, five years after this work was begun."[14]

Probably the most outstanding feature of these three catalogues
was the number of entries for parts of books and for articles in
periodicals. Fully half of the 300,000 entries in the Boston Athenaeum and Peabody Institute catalogues were of this type. Indeed,
their extent was such that in 1883, Cutter was distressed to learn

of Poole's proposal for an index of essays. "We have been somewhat surprised," he wrote, "to find no one pointing out that all
which he advocates has been already done in the catalogues of the
Boston Athenaeum, Brooklyn Library, and Peabody Institute."[15]
Still, the number of analytical entries in these two catalogues compared unfavorably with the number in the *Index-Catalogue*. In a
review of this work, George E. Wire noted that there were 511,112
entries for parts of publications, fully three times as many as
there were for whole publications.[16]

Such full and ably executed catalogues were to be had, however, only after tremendous expenditures of time and money. Work
on the Boston Athenaeum catalogue began in 1856; the first volume
did not appear until 1874, and the last not until 1882. The initial
volume of the first Peabody catalogue was published in 1883, some
fourteen years after work had begun; the final volume appeared
nine years later, in 1892. The Surgeon-General's catalogue was
begun in 1873, the first volume was published in 1880, the sixteenth
in 1895. In each instance, well over twenty years elapsed from
beginning to end. The full cost of the Athenaeum catalogue was
nearly $100,000; the cost of printing alone for the first Surgeon-
General's catalogue was $192,000.[17]

The foregoing experiences should have been an ominous warn-
ing for other libraries contemplating the publication of full dictionary catalogues. A few libraries, however, ignored the counsel. In
1880, Ellen Sawyer saw through the press an excellent catalogue of
the Massachusetts State Library, her only concession to costs being to include somewhat fewer periodical articles.[18] A similar
catalogue was prepared in 1889 for the Cleveland Public Library.[19]

THE MODIFIED ALPHABETICO-CLASSED CATALOGUES

In 1880, Stephen B. Noyes completed his excellent catalogue of
the Brooklyn Mercantile Library.[20] This catalogue was overshad-
owed by the monumental catalogues of the Boston Athenaeum, Peabody Institute, and Surgeon-General's Library only because they
indexed larger and more distinguished collections. Noyes had little
enthusiasm for the dictionary plan which these catalogues employed,
and especially for their almost complete reliance upon specific
subject entries. Concerning the Peabody catalogue he wrote:

> It seems to me a somewhat anomalous state of things that
> gentlemen who have displayed the utmost ingenuity in devising
> most elaborate and excellent systems for classifying books
> upon the shelves should nevertheless be content to have the
> disjecta membra of that classification scattered throughout
> four or five thousand pages of a printed catalogue.

I cannot admit that the average reader will find the system of specific subject entries altogether simple and intelligible....[21]

As the model for the Brooklyn catalogue, Noyes adopted the modified alphabetico-classed arrangement which Ezra Abbot had used at Harvard some years previously in the subject portion of the card catalogue. Noyes had first experimented with this form of arrangement in the two-volume subject catalogue of the Library of Congress printed in 1869, which he had planned and partly carried out. The Brooklyn catalogue went beyond either of these previous ventures, however, in that the author and title entries were interfiled in the same alphabetical sequence with the subject entries.

"The present Catalogue," wrote Noyes, "aims to afford readers a more or less systematic arrangement of authors, titles, subjects, and classes, in one general alphabet."[22] In preparing the subject portion of the catalogue, his procedure was to arrange related subjects whenever possible alphabetically under one of some thirty classes, each of which took its proper position in the alphabetical order. Certain subjects "too fragmentary or insulated, or on the other hand too complex and many sided"[23] were entered directly in the main alphabetical sequence. In providing entries for parts of books and for articles in periodicals, Noyes was quite as generous as the compilers of the Boston Athenaeum and Peabody Institute catalogues. An example in point is the class, "Biography." Of some 11,000 entries, only 3,000 were for whole works. In short, in over-all execution, fullness and accuracy of entries, cross references, and typographical appearance the Brooklyn catalogue had no superior.

Upon learning of the plan of the projected Brooklyn catalogue, Cutter had been disturbed by "this mixture of partial dictionary and incomplete classification."[24] He acknowledged, however, that "the selection of classes, though irregularly made, may be so contrived, (it is intended so to be,) as to correspond to the public's unsystematic association of ideas."[25] Cutter's second thoughts were the more accurate, for never was a catalogue more warmly received or more widely praised. In Justin Winsor's presidential address before the American Library Association in 1881, he called special attention to the catalogue and termed it "an admirable boon to all of us."[26]

The effect of Noyes's views upon the catalogues of his contemporaries was immediate. In 1878 Edward Capen, long connected with the Boston Public Library, prepared a catalogue modeled after the Brooklyn catalogue—although not so full—for the Public Library

of Haverhill, Massachusetts.[27] A similar catalogue was prepared
in 1882 by Frederic B. Perkins for the Fall River, Massachusetts,
Public Library.[28] Had Noyes not suffered an untimely death, he
would surely have exerted an even more significant influence upon
the development of American library catalogues.

THE CLASSED CATALOGUES

When Dewey appeared on the library scene at the beginning of
the final quarter of the nineteenth century, the fortunes of the
classed catalogue were at low ebb. Whatever the inherent advantages of logical classification were, "the impossibility of knowing,"
as Dewey phrased it, "just where to put a book in cataloguing, and
just where to look for it when it is wanted again"[29] had brought
even the most ardent supporters of the classed catalogue near despair. Adding to the troubles of the classed catalogue at that time
was the appearance of that model of the dictionary method, the
Boston Athenaeum Catalogue of 1874-82.

For Dewey a dictionary catalogue in any form was a drab
prospect at best. Since the dictionary method lacked any element
of logical classification, Dewey believed it must always have severe
limitations and that it was vastly inferior to a satisfactory classed
catalogue.[30] The task to Dewey, then, was clear—improve the
classed catalogue. *A Classification and Subject Index,*[31] which
Dewey devised for use in the Amherst College Library, was his
proposed solution.

The essential elements of Dewey's scheme, as he indicated by
his choice of title, were a subject classification and an alphabetical
subject index for that classification. His unique contribution, however, lay in his use of the notation system which he devised to accompany his subject classification. A notation system, of course,
is the network of symbols used to represent, in shorthand fashion,
the various classes and their subdivisions which make up the subject classification. Dewey's system, as every college freshman
knows, involves the use of a decimal notation.

For his alphabetical subject index, which he termed a "Relativ
Index" and considered the most important feature of his scheme,
Dewey compiled an extensive list of subjects, drawn from the leading catalogues and bibliographies of the day. Following each subject he listed, not the page in the catalogue where material on that
topic was to be found, or the shelf where the books were located,
but rather the decimal notation which indicated where material on
that particular topic had been placed in the subject classification.
This same decimal notation was also used as the basic element in
the book number and determined, of course, the physical location

of the book. By this simple device Dewey succeeded in making a single symbol reveal not only the subject of a book but also its location on the shelves. A valuable by-product of Dewey's system, although it was not original with him, was the substitution of a flexible and relative book location scheme for the conventional fixed location by shelf.

Dewey's system removed the strongest objections to the classed catalogue. After determining the subject of a book, the cataloguer could consult the "Relativ Index" to learn where in the subject classification books on that topic had been assigned. This procedure assured that different books on the same subject would be classed together, insofar as their content was correctly assessed. Similarly, a reader desiring a book on a particular topic needed but to find from the "Relativ Index" where the material on that subject had been placed. Although Dewey's system was designed primarily for use with a classed catalogue, it was chiefly used for quite another purpose—the arrangement of books and pamphlets upon shelves. Dewey installed his system immediately at Amherst in card form, but he was unable to prepare a similar catalogue in printed book form until 1904, in which year the second edition of the A.L.A. Catalog appeared under his editorship.[32] Other librarians, however, prepared printed book catalogues according to his methods considerably before that date.

The first complete application of Dewey's cataloguing ideas in a large, general library was made by Josephus Larned in 1877 in the Buffalo Young Men's Association Library.[33] The success of the system at Buffalo so impressed K. A. Linderfelt that in 1879 he decided to install it in the Milwaukee Public Library.[34] Work was immediately begun on a card catalogue which upon completion in 1885 was printed.[35] This constituted one of the first examples of a printed classed catalogue compiled in accordance with Dewey's ideas.

Linderfelt's catalogue consisted of three main divisions: (1) an alphabetical index of authors and anonymous and striking titles; (2) a classed list; and (3) an alphabetical index of subjects. The entries in the alphabetical list, unfortunately, did not provide the book number; for this information the reader was obliged to refer to the second sequence of entries, the main part of the catalogue. These entries, full and accurate, were classed roughly according to Dewey's subject classification, although in many instances Linderfelt employed a subject grouping which resulted in something other than a strict progression of Dewey numbers. The last part of the catalogue, the alphabetical index of subjects, was modeled quite closely upon Dewey's "Relativ Index." William C. Lane's review of Linderfelt's catalogue in the Library Journal exhibited respect, but hardly enthusiasm.[36] Those respects in which Linder-felt had deviated from Dewey somewhat lessened the usefulness of his catalogue.

Dewey's ideas were carried out much more faithfully and with correspondingly better results in a second catalogue published at this time. George Watson Cole, who would shortly be one of the first students to enroll in Dewey's School of Library Economy at Columbia College, compiled a model classed catalogue for the collections of the Fitchburg, Massachusetts, Public Library.[37] His classed catalogue, like the Milwaukee catalogue, was composed of three major divisions: an author index, a classified list, and an alphabetical index of subjects. The greatest improvement of Cole's catalogue over Linderfelt's was in the construction of the author index. In addition to the entries for authors and for anonymous and striking titles, there were entries for editors and translators. The entries were also fuller in that complete names of authors were given whenever possible, imprints were included, and book numbers added. Finally, unlike the Milwaukee catalogue, the main classified sequence of the Fitchburg catalogue was a faithful reproduction of the order of the Dewey subject classification.

The printed book catalogue had become almost a rarity before the first volume of the remarkable classed catalogue of the Pittsburgh Carnegie Library appeared in 1903.[38] At the time the plan of the catalogue was conceived, the librarian was Edwin H. Anderson, a future president of the American Library Association. Inasmuch as he was a former student of Dewey's, his choice of the classed arrangement was hardly surprising. For the task of supervising the preparation of the catalogue, Anderson secured the services of Miss Margaret Mann in 1902. This was a fortunate appointment. Because of its classed catalogues, wrote William Warner Bishop, "the Carnegie Library of Pittsburgh enjoys a peculiar distinction among American libraries—a distinction which it owes directly to Margaret Mann."[39]

The first catalogue, which established the form for those to follow, consisted of the usual main classified sequence, followed by an author index and an alphabetical index of subjects. The entries for the 145,000 volumes which were included in this first three-volume work provided less bibliographical detail than the entries in the Fitchburg catalogue. The entries in the author index, for example, contained only brief author and title transcriptions, date of publication, and book number. Also included was the number of the page in the main classified sequence where the entry was listed in full. The place of publication was omitted from the entries both in the author index and in the main classified sequence. The alphabetical index of subjects followed Dewey's "Relativ Index" quite closely. Miss Mann intended to furnish annotations for many of the titles, but only a few entries in the first part of the catalogue were thus supplied.

Although there were printed classed catalogues other than those described in the preceding paragraphs, they never became commonplace in American libraries. This is difficult to understand when one remembers that Dewey's system for constructing a classed catalogue removed the strongest objections to its use. Dewey himself, however, remained firm in his faith in the classed arrangement, in his belief that eventually it would come into its own, and in his opposition to the dictionary arrangement:

> I do not believe in the dictionary catalog. I have tried to be converted, but the more I am converted the less I believe in it. We have had valuable catalogs made on this system, but valuable because of the ability put into their making. The dictionary catalog has been a popular fad and will die out.[40]

To this Cutter countered:

> I feel just the opposite. The classed catalog is just now beginning to be a fad with librarians; it will have its run and then fall out of favor again. [41]

Whatever the merits of the two systems might be, it is certain that Cutter spoke with prophetic accuracy.

Such were the last attempts of libraries to publish full book catalogues of their collections on the dictionary, alphabetico-classed, and classed systems. If a single event were to be selected to mark the end of the full printed catalogue in book form, it should in all probability be the appearance in 1898 of James L. Whitney's "Considerations as to a Printed Catalogue in Book Form."[42] In this report Whitney, chief cataloguer of the Boston Public Library, set forth in carefully worded and well-documented form the reasons why that institution should not print its full catalogue. As of June, 1898, Whitney noted, a full catalogue of the collections of the Boston Public Library would consist of 1,250,000 entries, which would require, in printed form, about thirty volumes of one thousand pages each. If no entries were included for books received after printing had begun, from sixteen to twenty years would be required for the completion of the catalogue. At this time one million additional cards would have accumulated, and only one fourth of the books desired by readers would be represented in the printed portion of the catalogue. If copies of the catalogue were sold for their full cost, the number disposed of would be few; if they were sold for a nominal sum, the number would still be quite limited.

In view of the preceding considerations it is obvious that

Whitney believed any attempts to compute the full cost of such a catalogue were unnecessary. That the Boston Public Library, which had introduced so many innovations and improvements in the printed catalogue, should also write its final chapter seems only appropriate.

TECHNOLOGICAL DEVELOPMENTS

Throughout the latter half of the nineteenth century, librarians kept constant watch for the technological breakthrough that might enable them to retain their catalogues in the venerated and cherished printed book form. In Jewett's scheme for printing catalogues from individual stereotyped plates for each title, it appeared for a time the way had been cleared.[43] Subsequent events, of course, proved this hope to have been ill-founded. Some years later another occurrence—the invention of the linotype machine—provided librarians with renewed hope.

Linotype

Although by 1875 the rotary press and other developments in allied crafts had revolutionized much of the printing process, in one respect it was virtually unchanged—the setting of type. Since 1800 a succession of inventors had labored vainly to devise a mechanical and a faster means for composing type. Success was reserved for the efforts of an immigrant German watchmaker, Ottmar Mergenthaler, who conceived the brilliant idea of assembling individual matrices and casting molten metal into them to form single lines of type.[44] The tasks of composing, justifying, casting, and redistributing the matrices were all united in a single machine. In the individual lines of type which could be arranged, rearranged, stored, and used again, many librarians believed they saw a process admirably suited for the printing of catalogues.

Librarians, who had waited long and expectantly for just such a development, lost little time in investigating the possible uses of the linotype machine for their purposes. Although an earlier model of the linotype had been successfully employed in the *New York Tribune* offices in 1886, only after the appearance of the Simplex Linotype in 1890 would Mergenthaler agree that a satisfactory machine had been achieved.[45] Before the year was out, Ernest C. Richardson of the Princeton Library had entered into correspondence with the Linotype Company.[46] The following year, according to Richardson, a finding list of the New London, Connecticut, Public Library was printed by linotype.[47] Before another year passed, the Boston Public Library began to use linotype.[48] In 1893 the

Enoch Pratt Free Library printed the fifth edition of its *Finding List* by this means.[49] Even the venerable Cutter recommended in 1895 that linotype be used in the new Forbes Library he was building in Northampton, Massachusetts.[50]

How did libraries intend to employ the linotype, and what were the advantages expected from its use? The plans of the New Haven Free Public Library, although perhaps more comprehensive than those of some libraries, were not by any means atypical.[51] As each book was catalogued and added to the collections, a casting was made of the entry. Since the entry was limited in most instances to one line, the casting usually consisted of but a single bar of type. The bars, once made, had exceptional adaptability. Being quite durable, they could be sorted, shifted, arranged, rearranged, used repeatedly, and stored. New Haven, for example, intended to employ their linotype bars, successively, for printing catalogue cards, announcements of current additions in the local newspaper, bulletins of recent acquisitions, supplements to the printed catalogue, and, finally, a complete new edition of the general catalogue. The linotype process had other advantages. Since the type was a solid bar which could not become pied, it was not necessary to proof the slugs when using them a second time. Too, the investment of the library in type metal could be readily recovered since the bars could at any time be sold, melted down, and the lead reused.

The linotype process was not without its drawbacks—even in the eyes of its sponsors. Nathan Billstein of the Friedenwald Company wrote in 1894 that:

> The chief disadvantages of the method at present are the drawbacks in the use of characters not on the keyboard, the restrictions in the styles of type..., the short life of the cast, the superior preparation of manuscript required, and, perhaps, a partial sacrifice of some of the refinements of book-printing.[52]

Librarians would have added that for other than title-a-line catalogues, the linotype had another serious disadvantage. The castings for entries running to two or more lines consisted of a corresponding number of individual type bars. In operation these bars frequently became separated and could be assembled again only after much loss of time. Librarians also quickly learned that the expense of printing the first edition of a catalogue by linotype was little less than that of printing by conventional means; only in the printing of the second and subsequent editions, and then depending upon the number of new titles, was there a substantial saving.

The most serious objections to the use of linotype appeared

only after libraries had stored the bars following their initial use, and then attempted to employ them in the printing of a second catalogue. The cost of maintaining and storing extensive files of type bars, which it had been supposed would be nominal, was found to be substantial. Far more serious, however, was the fact that a large sum of money had to be tied up indefinitely in standing type. Finally, the interfiling of old and new type bars, especially when their numbers were large, frequently required as much labor as the setting of the entire catalogue anew.

The foregoing problems were all encountered by the Boston Public Library in their extensive use of linotyping. When considering linotype for the printing of their entire catalogue in 1898, they were forced to conclude:

> With the linotype as up to this time developed, methods which hold good for printing such a publication as the Annual List would cease to be operative in the case of a larger and certainly of a much larger catalogue. The cost of arrangement and editing would be out of all proportion to the increase of titles.

> ...Should the linotype ever through the progress of invention overcome its present limitations and effect that which now seems impossible, no one will rejoice more than the maker of catalogues. [53]

Thus, whereas the linotype had a definite usefulness for printing limited and frequently reissued title-a-line lists, it, too, was impracticable for printing full, general catalogues of libraries.

Rudolph's Blueprint Process

A new plan for printing catalogues which had far less to recommend it than the linotype was announced in the spring of 1899 by Alexander J. Rudolph, assistant librarian of the Newberry Library. Rudolph made far greater claims for his method than were ever advanced for linotype. His novel plan, he proclaimed, would enable libraries to publish "a complete catalog of their books at short periods, say every six months, or even at shorter intervals." [54] More importantly, "its wonderful simplicity makes it possible for each library to do its own printing."

Rudolph's scheme involved nothing more than the blueprint process. The copy to be reproduced was laid face up on a sheet of photosensitized paper, and the whole was then placed in direct sunlight. After proper exposure, the sensitized paper was washed in chemicals, and the familiar blue background with white characters

appeared. The advantages were those of any photographic method—
the faithful reproduction of the copy provided.

In 1899 Rudolph proposed that the blueprint method be used to
print a catalogue of the accessions of the British Museum Library
since 1880.[55] The books added during that period were not, of
course, represented in the great British Museum catalogue,[56] and
could be located only by searching through some four hundred separate printed lists of accessions. The plan was to clip the 900,000
entries in these lists, interfile them in one large alphabetical sequence, and then print them by means of the blueprint process.
Rudolph estimated that the finished work would run to some forty
volumes. One volume containing the entries for "Academies" was
actually produced in 1899.[57]

This first product of the Rudolph blueprint process was not too
kindly received by Charles Martel, who stated bluntly that the catalogue did "not warrant any claims of 'having done it.'"[58] Although
Martel was dissatisfied with the physical appearance of the volume,
his main criticisms centered around costs. The blueprint method,
he noted, was not an edition process and, hence, was uneconomical
for works wanted in more than a very few copies. Almost simultaneous with the appearance of Rudolph's catalogue came the announcement of the British Museum's plan to print a supplement.[59]
This, of course, rendered the continuation of Rudolph's work quite
unnecessary. The fact that the blueprint process was not considered for the printing of another catalogue demonstrated rather
conclusively that, once again, technology had been found wanting.

Rudolph Indexer

The blueprint process was by no means the only solution suggested by the resourceful Rudolph for the cataloguing problems
which beset libraries. As the meetings of the American Library
Association in San Francisco in 1891 were drawing to a close, one
of the host librarians, J. V. Cheney of the Public Library, took the
floor to make a dramatic announcement. Mr. A. J. Rudolph, now
first assistant at the San Francisco Public Library, was shortly
bringing out a new method of cataloguing, "the adoption of which
bids fair to amount to something like a revolution."[60] Because all
of the patents had not yet cleared, Cheney was not free to divulge
the exact nature of the machine. But he described in glowing terms
the benefits librarians could expect from it. This new invention,
he declared, would render obsolete the cumbrous card catalogue,
making the printing of catalogues and lists unnecessary; enable
librarians to discard their pens; accomplish the long-sought universal catalogue; and provide an accuracy and fullness in entries

hitherto impossible. In addition, all of these benefits could be obtained economically and with despatch, one assistant being able to
perform the work formerly done by five.

Because of the extraordinary nature of the claims made,
Cheney wisely took the precaution of showing the invention to the
highly respected president-elect of the Association, William I.
Fletcher. Although Fletcher was unwilling to guarantee that all of
the advantages claimed would be fully realized, he did state that he
would "probably claim as much for it if it was of my own contriv-
ance."[61] Despite the testimony of their respected President, the
delegates quite understandably departed for their homes in varying
states of disbelief and confusion.

This confusion was dispelled in part the following year at the
Lakewood Conference of the American Library Association when
President Fletcher described the invention in some detail.[62] Most
librarians, however, were not privileged to see the invention itself
until the next year at the World's Library Congress in Chicago.
There it was reported to be the outstanding attraction of the meetings.[63] Librarians shortly learned that the invention was not a new
method of cataloguing at all; rather, it was a new means of presenting the catalogue, once made, to the readers.

The Rudolph Indexer, as the invention was termed, was truly
an ingenious device. Its basic element was a sheet of pressboard,
16 inches by 4 inches, with metal edges grooved for the ready re-
ceipt of entries in card or slip form. Some 350 of these pressboards, joined together in an endless chain, were stacked compactly
in the lower portion of a wood cabinet 42 inches high, 20 inches
deep, and 30 inches wide. Near the top of the cabinet were two
hexagonal drums over which the file of pressboards could be drawn,
in either direction, by the revolution of a crank. Through a plate-
glass cover on top of the machine five of the pressboards could be
viewed at one time as they passed over the top of the drums. Each
pressboard accommodated about thirty-five entries averaging four
lines in length. Thus, the capacity of the machine was about 12,000
entries, of which 175 could be viewed at one time.

What was the reaction of librarians to the Rudolph Indexer? It
was apparent to all except the most naive that the original claims
made for the machine could in no way be substantiated. Nevertheless, librarians quickly recognized that the Indexer appeared to
have some of the advantages of both the printed book catalogue—
the simultaneous viewing of many titles—and of the card catalogue—
the facility of being kept current. Very shortly the Indexers were
purchased, or being considered for purchase, by several libraries.
William C. Lane, in his survey of cataloguing practices in 1893,
found that experiments were already being made with the machines

in the Brooklyn Library, Detroit Public, New Haven Free Public, Newberry, Enoch Pratt, Stanford University, Oakland Public in California, and, of course, Rudolph's own San Francisco Free Public.[64] Lane also noted that the merits of the Indexer were such that Cutter was considering its introduction in the Forbes Library in Northampton, Massachusetts.

Disillusionment came fast. In 1898, George E. Wire, in his "Report on Classification and Cataloging" delivered at the Chautauqua Conference of the American Library Association, noted that "the Rudolph Indexer, from which so much was expected, ... has failed even in its new home." [65] Wire had reference to the Newberry Library where Cheney and Rudolph had recently gone as librarian and assistant librarian respectively. The Indexer had a fatal defect which was immediately evident: it could be used by but one person at a time which, of course, tied up the entries for some 12,000 titles. The Indexer was also expensive and lacked the flexibility and ease of interfiling and rearranging entries possessed by the card catalogue. Nor did it have the printed book catalogue's virtues of being available outside the library and in multiple copies. Nevertheless, for a short period of time, even in the minds of the ablest librarians of that day, the Rudolph Indexer was a worthy challenger of both printed book and card catalogues. The significance of the Rudolph Indexer lay in its attempts to retain what was probably the greatest virtue of the printed book catalogue—the facility for the simultaneous viewing of many entries.

THE FINDING LIST

Many librarians, despairing of printing full book catalogues by existing means and impatient with waiting for technological miracles, adopted a modified version of the printed catalogue—the finding list. Introduced about 1875, the finding list was nothing more than the familiar printed catalogue in a very abbreviated form. Some type of printed book catalogue was still held to be desirable, especially for the public and other large circulating libraries. Whereas these libraries would certainly have preferred the fuller printed catalogue, they were hopeful that the brief and inexpensive finding list, used in conjunction with the increasingly acceptable full catalogue on cards, might prove to be adequate.

The finding list was in some respects a revival of the brief printed catalogue of the colonial period and early years of the nineteenth century. The primary purpose of each was to show whether a particular title was in the library and, if so, where. There was, however, a basic difference in the thinking underlying their preparation. In the early years of the nineteenth century, the

primary and almost sole purpose of the catalogue was to serve as
a finding list; by the latter years of the century, the function of the
catalogue had, of course, been greatly extended.

The reintroduction of the finding list into American libraries
was not entirely by design. In May of 1874 the doors of the new
Chicago Public Library were opened, prematurely in the opinion of
its librarian, William F. Poole. Although there were more than
17,000 books on the shelves, there had been neither time nor funds
for the preparation of a printed catalogue. It is doubtful whether it
would have been wise to prepare one in any event, for scarcely a
third of the books ordered had been received. In order to obtain
some form of a guide for his readers quickly and inexpensively,
the resourceful Poole decided to print the shelf list. In July the
first of his widely heralded finding lists of the Chicago Public Library appeared.[66] Its arrangement was that of the books on the
shelves, alphabetically by author under several broad subjects.
The entries themselves could not have been briefer, consisting
merely of the surname of the author, short title, and book number.
Armed with this brief finding list and a card catalogue accessible
to readers only through the library staff, the Chicago Public Library, Poole boasted, "has, in the first two months after its opening, taken rank, as to its circulation, with the largest and most
successful public libraries of the country." [67]

Poole's finding list was an immediate success. Despite its
brevity it was found to answer satisfactorily the majority of inquiries made by users of the Chicago Public Library. For those
questions it failed to answer, immediate recourse could be had to
the more complete catalogue on cards. Revised editions of the
finding list appeared in rapid succession in 1875 and 1876.[68] Following the appearance of the latter list, Poole noted with obvious
satisfaction:

> No library list of 50,000 volumes was ever before fur-
> nished at this low price [fifteen cents] without loss. It is so
> cheap that the public will buy it, and they will not buy an ex-
> pensive catalogue. Several other libraries have adopted the
> plan in lieu of a more elaborate and costly catalogue.[69]

Nevertheless, Poole was still not completely satisfied. "The Finding Lists now in use," he observed, "furnish only an imperfect and
incomplete substitute [for the full printed catalogue]."[70] Any lin-
gering doubts he may have had concerning the value of his finding
lists, however, were removed by three more editions, published in
1878, 1880, and 1884. The following conclusive statement was
made by Poole in his annual report for 1885:

> In connection with our card catalogue, ... the Finding list
> seems to fully meet the demands of the public for a printed
> inventory of the books, and it practically answers one of the
> most controverted and difficult questions which has arisen in
> the administration of rapidly growing libraries with large con-
> stituencies of book-borrowers: "How can readers best be
> served with late and frequently-revised lists of books contained
> in the library?"[71]

The finding list, being but an abbreviated version of the full
printed catalogue, eventually appeared in a comparable—indeed,
almost the same—variety of forms. From Poole's pioneering efforts at the Chicago Public Library, however, the finding list did
acquire a predominant and characteristic form. Poole's initial
finding list, it will be recalled, was merely a copy of the shelf list.
To the simple classed sequence of entries thus formed, he eventually added an alphabetical index of subjects. The sixth edition of
his list, published in 1884, was so constructed. The entries, one
to a line, remained extremely brief. They consisted of the author's
surname, short title, and the book number, and were arranged alphabetically by author under the various classes and subclasses.
Cross references, entries for parts of books, and notes listing the
contents of books were rarely used. Finding lists were prepared
according to this general plan in countless libraries during the last
quarter of the nineteenth century. Typical were the finding lists
prepared by the Minneapolis Public Library in 1890 and the Bloomington, Illinois, and Decatur, Illinois, Public libraries in 1894.[72]

The dictionary arrangement was employed upon occasion in
the preparation of finding lists. In 1880, William Foster published
a list of the holdings of the Providence Public Library in which
author and title entries were interfiled in a single sequence.[73]
Similar lists were prepared by the Galesburg, Illinois, Public Library in 1887, and by the Los Angeles Public Library in 1891.[74]
The finding list which George Watson Cole had printed for the collections of the Jersey City Public Library in 1891 included not only
author and title entries but also subject entries and cross references.[75] Louisa Cutler prepared one of the most elaborate finding
lists for the Utica, New York, Public Library in 1895.[76] It consisted of an alphabetically arranged sequence of author and title
entries, a classified sequence of entries, and an alphabetical index
of subjects. Clearly, the line between the full printed catalogue
and the printed finding list was not sharply drawn.

By the end of the nineteenth century the finding list was widely
employed in American libraries. William I. Fletcher observed in
1894 that "the more common practice now is to maintain good

written catalogues, kept well up-to-date, and to issue occasionally, temporary and cheaply made lists of new books, or of works in special classes."[77] George E. Wire reported to his colleagues at the American Library Association Conference in 1898 that "the finding list is coming more and more to the fore, and the catalog as a printed aid is going into the background."[78] Although the objections to the full printed book catalogue were not removed by the finding list, they were considerably lessened. Because of its brevity the finding list could be prepared and printed more cheaply and could be reissued at more frequent intervals. Nevertheless, its cost was still substantial, and within a very few years the finding list, like the full printed catalogue, would be superseded by the printed library card.

COOPERATIVE EFFORTS WITHIN THE AMERICAN LIBRARY ASSOCIATION

In October of 1876 more than one hundred librarians had gathered in Philadelphia to form the American Library Association. Prominent, perhaps even paramount, among their reasons for organizing was their anxiety about the difficulties and costs of cataloguing. They hoped to resolve cooperatively some of the many cataloguing problems that had defied them individually. One of their first acts was the formation of a Cooperation Committee under the chairmanship of Charles A. Cutter.[79] Although the Committee addressed itself to all aspects of library cooperation, cooperation in cataloguing was the chief consideration from the beginning.

Various articles published in the early numbers of the new *Library Journal* and several proposals made at the first conference furnished additional evidence of the deep concern of librarians for their catalogues. In the initial issue of the *Library Journal*, published a month before the formation of the American Library Association, Charles A. Nelson commented on a plan described in *Publishers' Weekly* for "the supplying by publishers of slips containing the titles of new books with a synopsis of their contents, for the guidance of purchasers and the convenience of librarians."[80] In that same issue Dewey noted in an article on "Public Documents" that "the first great need ... is some full index, brought up and kept up to date."[81] Before the first volume of the *Library Journal* was complete, Dewey had also introduced a plan which eventually resulted in the *Catalog of "A.L.A." Library*.[82] During the conference Poole presented a proposal which ultimately produced a revision of his *Index to Periodical Literature*.[83] Finally, at these same meetings Dewey introduced the subject of "the preparation of printed

titles for the common use of libraries" and successfully moved
that a plan to accomplish this end be formulated.[84]

The foregoing published articles illustrate the two approaches
the Association adopted in its efforts to resolve the cataloguing
impasse. The first involved the preparation and publication,
largely through the voluntary cooperation of librarians, of bibliographies and indexes of particular classes of library materials. It
was hoped, of course, that these publications would relieve individual libraries of the necessity of preparing extensive subject catalogues. The second approach centered around efforts to devise a
broad system of cooperative or centralized cataloguing, and resulted ultimately in the Library of Congress program of preparing,
printing, and distributing library cards.

One of the developments which magnified the costs of preparing and printing book catalogues was, of course, the providing of an
ever more extensive approach to the subject content of collections.
This practice was early challenged on the ground that such was the
proper function of subject bibliographies and indexes. One of the
most ardent and articulate champions of this point of view was
William I. Fletcher. "No practice current in libraries," he declared, "seems to me more open to the charge of superstition than
the blind following of the practice of loading our catalogs with ana-
lyticals, when our eyes ought to be open to the new era of bibliographies and indexes."[85] Fletcher's words were admittedly intem-
perate, as were many of the writings on this subject at the time;
nevertheless, librarians generally recognized that there were certain types and classes of publications which could be handled more
effectively in published bibliographies than in the subject catalogue
of each individual library. Indeed, this precise idea prompted the
formation of the Publishing Section of the American Library Association in 1886.[86]

Poole's Index

The pioneer effort to segregate certain types of library materials for treatment in published bibliographies and indexes occurred some time before the founding of the American Library
Association and long before the formation of its Publishing Section.
Reference has been made to the publication in 1848 of the first edition of *Poole's Index to Periodical Literature*.[87] Because libraries
had many of the periodicals indexed and because they had been unable to analyze them in their catalogues, *Poole's Index* was an immediate success. The result of Poole's efforts was that during the
next twenty years libraries made little attempt, with but rare exception, to include the contents of periodicals in their catalogues.[88]

Poole's Index was revised and brought up to date in 1853;[89] however, even this edition was badly out of date when American librarians gathered in Philadelphia in 1876, and high on their list of
things to be accomplished was a revision of the *Index*. Accordingly,
when Poole proposed a plan for the cooperative compilation of a
new edition, it was enthusiastically accepted, and a committee consisting of Poole, Winsor, and Cutter was appointed to superintend
publication.[90] In 1882 the long-awaited new edition of *Poole's Index*
appeared.[91] As a result of Poole's and other periodical indexes,
American libraries to this day have found it unnecessary to analyze
the contents of periodicals in their catalogues.

A.L.A. Index

At the American Library Association Conference in 1882, the
indefatigable Poole, having just sent the manuscript for his *Index*
to the printers, was ready with another project for the consideration of his colleagues. His suggestion was that they jointly analyze
and index "volumes of essays and miscellanies, and standard books
in history, biography, political economy, social science, education,
etc." [92] Although this material was vaguely defined, much of it was
to be found in almost every library, and in few libraries was it adequately catalogued. Poole's proposal was quickly accepted, and
the *A.L.A. Index* appeared some ten years later under the editorship of William I. Fletcher.[93] Today the well-known *Essay and
General Literature Index* covers much the same area. Again, it
has been possible for libraries to omit a sizable and useful block
of materials from their catalogues.

Publications of the Federal Government

The publications of the national government constituted another
class of materials well adapted for treatment in published bibliographies. Almost every library had at least a small documents collection which seldom was adequately indexed. From its inception
the American Library Association evinced a strong interest in the
cataloguing and distribution of documents. At the second meeting
of the Association, President Winsor appointed a special Documents
Committee.[94] Although the initial concern of the Committee was
with the distribution of documents, by 1881 it was recommending
the annual issuance of "a list of all publications ordered to be
printed by authority of Congress, or the departments." [95] The present system of listing and indexing government publications is in no
small part the result of the continuous interest of the Association
through the years.

A.L.A. Catalog

In 1877, Dewey proposed that the Association compile and publish a carefully selected list of some 10,000 volumes which might well form the nucleus of a small public library.[96] This list, Dewey argued, would serve as an aid and a guide to readers, book buyers, and librarians alike; most important, however, it would "remove the necessity of that greatest terror of librarians and finance committees of the smaller and poorer libraries, the printed catalog."[97] Fifteen years elapsed before the *Catalog of "A.L.A." Library* appeared.[98] There is slight evidence that many public libraries ever used it as a catalogue of their collections; nevertheless, the *Catalog* represented another attempt to identify a special class of materials which might be handled most efficiently by means of a printed bibliography.

The preparation of published bibliographies and indexes for special classes of materials accomplished two things for libraries. First, it enabled them to have, at slight cost, printed lists for significant segments of their collections. From the standpoint of the individual library these lists had the usual shortcomings of all printed bibliographies: some items in the library were not in the lists, and some items in the lists were not in the library. Second, the portion of the catalogue which remained for each library to compile was significantly lessened; however, it was still too large for the individual library to print, or even to compile in manuscript. Librarians were slowly realizing that nothing short of a broad and comprehensive program of cooperative cataloguing would solve the problem.

Printed Catalogue Cards

It would be difficult to document when thoughtful librarians first began to ponder the futility and waste of countless libraries cataloguing the same books. Jewett was certainly aware of the problem in 1853 when he made his proposal for stereotyping catalogues at the Smithsonian Institution. His colleagues' enthusiasm for the plan and their bitter disappointment at its failure would seem to indicate that they, too, were genuinely disturbed by the problem. According to Dewey a successful program of cooperative or centralized cataloguing was the greatest benefit which the founders of the American Library Association hoped to realize from their organization.[99] At the very first meeting of the Association, Dewey was on his feet calling for a plan for "the preparation of printed titles for the common use of libraries."[100] Dewey was frank in admitting his uncertainty about the form the plan might take:

Who shall prepare the titles of new books as published?
The Library of Congress or its copyright department? The
publishers themselves? A cataloguing bureau, established
and maintained by the libraries of the country? An individual
or firm, as a commercial venture? [101]

Actually, before the successful launching of the Library of Congress program, each of the other three possibilities was tried and
proved inadequate.

At the American Library Association Conference the succeeding year, 1877, President Winsor appointed a Committee on Title
Slips consisting of Bowker, Dewey, and himself to formulate a
plan. Their proposal, submitted the following year, was for publishers to forward a copy of each book printed, together with one
dollar, to the offices of *Publishers' Weekly*.[102] There, under the
guidance of Winsor and Cutter, catalogue cards would be prepared,
printed, and shipped to subscribing libraries. In their report for
1879, the Committee reluctantly acknowledged that their plan did
not appear to be feasible; they were ready, however, with another
proposal.[103]

Their second suggestion was that a list of all new books regis-
tered with *Publishers' Weekly* be printed on one side of thin paper
and forwarded monthly to librarians as a supplement of the *Library
Journal*. This list, known as the *Title Slip Registry,* would be
available in multiple copies, which could be clipped and the individual entries mounted on cards. Because of lack of support from
libraries, *Publishers' Weekly* announced the discontinuance of this
project a year later.[104]

The next venture in centralized cataloguing was no longer
lived. In 1887 the Publishing Section of the American Library Association announced an experimental plan under which catalogue
cards would be supplied, for one dollar, for one hundred leading
publications appearing during the last four months of the year.[105]
Once again, libraries failed to respond, and the project came to
nothing.

Another scheme for centralized cataloguing did not appear until 1893, in which year two plans were announced simultaneously.[106]
One involved the intentions of the Rudolph Indexer Company to sup-
ply printed cards for all books currently published in America and,
indeed, for entire libraries on contract. Cutter, who had just resigned from the Boston Athenaeum, was to be in charge of the program. This ambitious scheme never materialized, probably because of a second plan announced at this time by the Library Bureau of the American Library Association. Under the latter arrangement advance copies of currently published books were to be

solicited from publishers, and cards prepared and distributed to
subscribing libraries twice a week. This scheme—and modifications of it—was continued with indifferent success by the Library
Bureau until 1896, at which time responsibility was assumed by
the Publishing Section of the American Library Association.[107]
Under the new auspices the plan fared little better.

Although the causes for the failure of the foregoing programs
were not always clear, a few facts did emerge. For most libraries
the acceptance of any of the various plans would have required
basic and far-reaching changes in their normal cataloguing practices. In view of this librarians were understandably reluctant to
support a scheme unless they felt assured that it was permanent
and that it would furnish cards promptly for most of the books
added to their collections.

After considering at great length how such a program might
be formulated, the Co-operation Committee presented the following
recommendation at the 1900 Conference of the Association:

> That it ⌜the Association⌝ form under the direction of its
> Publishing Section a bureau for the co-operative cataloging
> and printing of cards under guarantee, which bureau shall un-
> dertake to catalog promptly or to provide for the cataloging of
> all books referred to it by co-operating libraries, shall print
> cards for the same and also any titles sent to it by co-operat-
> ing libraries, shall keep on file electrotypes of these titles for
> printing titles to order for libraries in general, shall publish
> regularly or from time to time a list of the titles in type or to
> be printed ... and shall be under the direct administration of
> an officer of the Publishing Section and the librarians of the
> guaranteeing libraries.[108]

This proposal of the Co-operation Committee was never put to
the test, for within a few months Herbert Putnam announced the
plans of the Library of Congress for the preparation, printing, and
distribution of catalogue cards among the libraries of the country.
From almost the inception of this program, American librarians
recognized that their long-awaited program of centralized cataloguing was at hand, and that the search for a successor to the
venerated printed book catalogue was finally at an end.

Notes

INTRODUCTION

1. An approach was made by Charles A. Cutter in his excellent article, "Library Catalogues," which appeared in U.S. Bureau of Education, *Public Libraries in the United States of America: Their History, Condition, and Management*, Special Report, Part I (Washington: Govt. Print. Off., 1876), p.526-622; article cited hereafter by title only. Although Cutter was concerned with all aspects of cataloguing, his remarks on book catalogues were especially full and informative, including a listing of more than one thousand printed catalogues. Dorothy M. Norris' *A History of Cataloguing and Cataloguing Methods, 1100-1850: With an Introductory Survey of Ancient Times* (London: Grafton, 1939) is also quite useful but, unfortunately, it is limited to libraries in England.

   In recent years two other interesting monographs have appeared on the subject of book catalogues; neither, however, has been primarily concerned with the effectiveness of the book catalogue as a device for listing the holdings of libraries. In 1956, Sears Jayne's *Library Catalogues of the English Renaissance* (Berkeley: Univ. of California Pr., 1956) appeared, and in the following year Archer Taylor's *Book Catalogues: Their Varieties and Uses* (Chicago: Newberry Library, 1957). In each work the chief purpose of the author was to prepare a guide to the contents of book catalogues for the modern bibliographer and scholar.

2. Robert E. Kingery and Maurice F. Tauber have just recently published a study on the book catalogue, containing several reprinted and several original articles, which emphasizes the events of recent years: *Book Catalogs*, ed. by Robert E. Kingery and Maurice F. Tauber (New York: Scarecrow Pr., 1963).

3. Charles C. Jewett, *Appendix to the Report of the Board of Regents of the Smithsonian Institution: Containing a Report on the Public Libraries, January 1, 1850* (31st Cong., 1st Sess., House Miscellaneous, No. 50 [Washington: Printed for the House of Reps., 1850]), p.4. Cited hereafter by title only.

4. G. K. Hall and Company, *Catalogue of Reference Works, January, 1963* (Boston: The Company, 1963).

I. THE PRINTED BOOK CATALOGUE IN COLONIAL AMERICA

1. Harvard University Library, *Catalogus librorum Bibliothecae Collegij Harvardini quod est Cantabrigiae in Nova Anglia* (Bostoni Nov-Anglorum: typis B. Green, 1723).
2. Ruth French Strout, "The Development of the Catalog and Cataloging Codes," *Library Quarterly*, 26:274 (Oct., 1956).
3. Konrad Gesner, *Bibliotheca universalis* (Zurich: Christophorus Froschoverus, 1545).
4. —— *Pandectarum sive partitionum universalium* (Zurich: Christophorus Froschoverus, 1548).
5. Florian Trefler, *Methodus exhibens per varios indices, et classes subinde quorumlibet librorum, cuiuslibet bibliothecae, breve, facilem, imitabilem ordinationem* (Augsburg: P. Ulhardum, 1560).
6. Andrew Maunsell, *Catalogue of English Printed Books* (London: A. Maunsell, 1595).
7. Leyden, Rijksuniversiteit, Bibliotheek, *Nomenclator auctorum omnium, quorum libri exstant in bibliotheca academiae Lugduno-Batavae, cum epistola de ordine ejus atque usu* (Leyden: 1595).
8. Augsburg, Bibliotheca Augustana, *Bibliothecae inclytae reip. Augustanae utriusque tum graecae tum latinae librorum & impressorum & manu exaratorum catalogus* (Augsburg: 1600).
9. Oxford University, Bodleian Library, *Catalogus librorum bibliothecae publicae quam vir ornatissimus Thomas Bodleius eques auratus in Academia Oxoniensi nuper instituit* (Oxford: J. Barnesium, 1605).
10. —— —— *Catalogus universalis librorum in bibliotheca Bodleiana* (Oxford: J. Short, 1620).
11. —— —— *Appendix ad. catalogum librorum in bibliotheca Bodleiana* (Oxford: 1635).
12. Augsburg, Bibliotheca Augustana, *Catalogus bibliothecae reipublicae Augustanae* (Augsburg: 1633).
13. Leyden, Rijksuniversiteit, Bibliotheek, *Catalogus bibliothecae publicae Lugduno-Batavae* (Leyden: 1640).
14. Oxford University, Bodleian Library, *Catalogus impressorum librorum bibliothecae Bodleianae in Academia Oxoniensi* (Oxford: 1674).
15. —— —— *Catalogus* ... (1605). Throughout the remainder of this study, general references are repeatedly made to the same catalogue. In order not to lengthen the manuscript unduly, the following procedure has been adopted: The first time the catalogue is mentioned, it is cited in a footnote. Subsequent references to the same catalogue take the form of noting in the text both the date of the catalogue's publication and the name of the library for which it was compiled; but no footnote citation is provided. This procedure applies, of course, only for general references to the catalogues; for references to specific pages or parts of catalogues the usual footnote citation is given.
16. Dorothy M. Norris, *A History of Cataloguing and Cataloguing Methods, 1100-1850: With an Introductory Survey of Ancient Times* (London: Grafton, 1939), p.148.
17. Louis Shores, *Origins of the American College Library, 1638-1800* (New York: Barnes & Noble, 1935), p.51.
18. Albert Predeek, *A History of Libraries in Great Britain and North America;* tr. by Lawrence S. Thompson (Chicago: American Library Association, 1947), p.18.
19. Alfred Hessel, *A History of Libraries;* tr. by Reuben Peiss (Washington, D.C.: Scarecrow Pr., 1950), p.75.

20. Shores, *op. cit.*, p.50.
21. Thomas Wright, *Literary Culture in Early New England, 1620-1730* (New Haven: Yale Univ. Pr., 1920), p.25-61, 110-36, 174-96; Samuel Eliot Morison, *The Intellectual Life of Colonial New England* (2d ed.; New York: New York Univ. Pr., 1956), p.113-32; Louis B. Wright, *The Cultural Life of the American Colonies, 1607-1763* (New York: Harper, 1957), p.126-53.
22. Shores, *op. cit.*, p.109.
23. "Holyoke Code of 1765," Colonial Society of Massachusetts, *Publications*, 31:369-75 (1935).
24. Charles Seymour Thompson, *Evolution of the American Public Library, 1653-1876* (Washington, D.C.: Scarecrow Pr., 1952), p.54.
25. Jesse Hauk Shera, *Foundations of the Public Library: The Origins of the Public Library Movement in New England, 1629-1855* (Chicago: Univ. of Chicago Pr., 1949), p.39.
26. "Harvard College Records: College Book IV," Colonial Society of Massachusetts, *Publications*, 16:467 (1925).
27. Princeton University Library, *A Catalogue of Books in the Library of the College of New Jersey, January 29, 1760* (Woodbridge: Printed by James Parker, 1760), p.iv.
28. Yale University Library, *A Catalogue of the Library of Yale-College in New Haven* (New London, Conn.: T. Green, 1743).
29. Library Company of Philadelphia, *A Catalogue of Books* . . . (Philadelphia: B. Franklin, 1741), p.56.
30. Princeton University Library, *A Catalogue of Books* . . . (1760), p.iii.
31. Thomas Clap, *The Annals or History of Yale-College* . . . (New Haven: Printed for J. Hotchkiss & B. Mecom, 1766), p.43.
32. Loganian Library, *Catalogus Bibliothecae Loganianae* . . . (Philadelphia: Printed by Peter Miller, 1760).
33. Philadelphia Association Library Company, *A Catalogue of Books* . . . (Philadelphia: Printed by William Bradford, 1765).
34. Library Company of Philadelphia, *The Charter, Laws, and Catalogue of Books* . . . (Philadelphia: Printed by Joseph Crukshank, 1770).
35. Harvard University Library, *Catalogus librorum in Bibliotheca cantabrigiensi selectus, frequentiorem in usum Harvardinatum, qui gradu baccalaurei in artibus nondum sunt donati* (Boston: Edes & Gill, 1773).
36. Library Company of Philadelphia, *The Charter, Laws, and Catalogue of Books* . . . (Philadelphia: B. Franklin & D. Hall, 1757).
37. —— *The Charter, Laws, and Catalogue of Books* . . . (Philadelphia: Printed by B. Franklin & D. Hall, 1764).
38. Redwood Library and Athenaeum, *A Catalogue of the Books* . . . (Newport: Printed by S. Hall, 1764).
39. Julian P. Boyd, "Foreword," Princeton University Library, *A Catalogue of Books in the Library of the College of New Jersey, January 29, 1760. Published by Order of the Trustees at Woodbridge, New Jersey, by James Parker* (Princeton: Reprinted by the Friends of the Library, 1949), p.[6].
40. The pressmarks were in the left-hand margin in Harvard University Library, *Catalogus* . . . (1723) and in its supplements printed in 1725 and 1735. In Harvard University Library, *Catalogus* . . . (1773), the pressmarks were found in the right-hand margin, as they were in Yale University Library, *A Catalogue* . . . (1743) and Yale University Library, *A Catalogue* . . . (New Haven: Printed by James Parker, 1755).
41. See, for example, Library Company of Philadelphia, *The Charter, Laws, and Catalogue* . . . (1770); or Loganian Library, *Catalogus* . . . (1760).
42. Shores, *op. cit.*, p.270-71.

43. Alfred C. Potter, "The Harvard College Library, 1723-1735," Colonial So-
    ciety of Massachusetts, *Transactions,* 35:3 (1924).
44. Ruth Schley, "Cataloging in the Libraries of Princeton, Columbia and Uni-
    versity of Pennsylvania before 1876" (unpublished master's thesis, School
    of Library Service, Columbia Univ., 1946), p.53.
45. Boyd, *op. cit.,* p.₍1₎.
46. Yale University Library, *A Catalogue* ... (1743), p.i-ii.
47. Library Company of Philadelphia, *Catalogue* ... (Philadelphia: Printed by
    B. Franklin, 1733). Citation from Charles Evans, *American Bibliography,*
    No. 3714. No copy of this catalogue is known to have survived.
48. —— *Catalogue* ... (Philadelphia: Printed by B. Franklin, 1735). Citation
    from Charles Evans, *American Bibliography,* No. 3950. No copy of this
    catalogue is known to have survived.
49. "Harvard College Records: College Book IV," Colonial Society of Massa-
    chusetts, *Publications,* 16:476 (1925).
50. Austin Baxter Keep, *History of the New York Society Library* (New York:
    De Vinne Pr., 1908), p.187. The catalogue referred to is *The Charter, and
    Bye-Laws, of the New-York Society Library: With a Catalogue of the Books*
    ... (New York: H. Gaine, 1773).
51. Letter from Edwin Wolf, II, Librarian of the Library Company of Philadel-
    phia, Sept. 4, 1958.
52. "Harvard College Records: College Book IV," Colonial Society of Massa-
    chusetts, *Publications,* 16:502-3 (1925).
53. Thompson, *op. cit.,* p.54. Only the Library Company of Philadelphia, the
    Redwood Library of Newport, the Philadelphia Association Library Company,
    the Providence Library, and the Philadelphia Union Library Company printed
    catalogues during the colonial period according to Charles A. Cutter, "Li-
    brary Catalogues," p.577. It is known, however, that both the Charleston Li-
    brary Society and the New York Society Library also published catalogues
    before the Revolution.
54. New York Society Library, *A Catalogue of the Books* ... (New York: H.
    Gaine, ₍1758₎).
55. —— *A Catalogue of the Books*... (New York: H. Gaine, ₍1761₎).
56. Charleston Library Society, *A Catalogue of Books* ... (Charlestown: Printed
    for the Society by R. Wells, 1770).

II. BEGINNINGS OF MODERN CATALOGUES, 1780-1850

1. John S. Brubacher and Willis Rudy, *Higher Education in Transition: An
   American History, 1636-1956* (New York: Harper, 1958), p.15.
2. *Ibid.,* p.172.
3. *Ibid.,* p.82.
4. *Ibid.,* p.63.
5. James Hulme Canfield, "The College Library," *Outlook,* 71:248 (May 24,
   1902).
6. Charles C. Jewett, "Second Report of the Assistant Secretary of the Smithsonian Institution, Relative to the Library—Presented Jan. 2, 1850," *Fourth
   Annual Report of the Board of Regents of the Smithsonian Institution... 1849*
   (31st Cong., 1st Sess., House Miscellaneous, No. 50 ₍Washington: 1850₎),
   p.32. Cited hereafter by title only.
7. Astor Library, *Alphabetical Index* ... (New York: R. Craighead, 1849), p.xx-
   xxii.
8. Brough, *op. cit.,* p.14-15.

9. Charles C. Jewett, *Appendix to the Report of the Board of Regents of the Smithsonian Institution, Containing a Report on the Public Libraries, January 1, 1850*, p.59.
10. —— "Second Report of the Assistant Secretary of the Smithsonian Institution, Relative to the Library—Presented Jan. 2, 1850," p.39.
11. The information in this paragraph was taken from Brough, *op. cit.*, p.14-15.
12. Columbia University, Philolexian Society, *Constitution, Catalogue of Library, and List of Members* . . . (New York: 1825), p.3.
13. Catharine P. Storie, "What Contribution Did the American College Society Library Make to the College Library? A Supplementary Chapter in the History of the American College Library" (unpublished master's thesis, School of Library Service, Columbia Univ., 1938), p.77-78.
14. Charles C. Jewett, "Second Report of the Assistant Secretary of the Smithsonian Institution, Relative to the Library—Presented Jan. 2, 1850," p.40.
15. —— *Appendix to the Report of the Board of Regents of the Smithsonian Institution, Containing a Report on the Public Libraries, January 1, 1850*, p.26, 84.
16. *Ibid.*, p.66, 81, 84, 169.
17. *Ibid.*, p.26, 84.
18. Quoted in Jesse Hauk Shera, *Foundations of the Public Library: The Origins of the Public Library Movement in New England, 1629-1855* (Chicago: Univ. of Chicago Pr., 1949), p.78.
19. Albert Predeek, *A History of Libraries in Great Britain and North America;* tr. by Lawrence S. Thompson (Chicago: American Library Association, 1947), p.94.
20. Quoted in Shera, *op. cit.*, p.207-8.
21. Philadelphia Mercantile Library Company, *Catalogue of the Books* . . . (Philadelphia: 1840), p.xiii.
22. New York Mercantile Library Association, *Systematic Catalogue of Books* . . . (New York: Harper, 1837), p.v.
23. Allegheny College Library, *Catalogus bibliothecae collegii Alleghaniensis* (Meadville, Pa.: T. Atkinson, 1823), p.136.
24. A committee of the proprietors of the Providence Athenaeum estimated "the cost of printing 500 copies of a catalogue 400 pages, in a style equal to that of the Brown University Catalogue, to be $490" (Providence Athenaeum, *Fourteenth Annual Report* . . . *1849*, p.11).
25. "Eleventh Annual Report . . . 1831," *Annual Reports of the Board of Directors of the Mercantile Library Association of the City of New York, from 1821 to 1838* (New York: 1868), p.71.
26. Ezra Abbot, ". . . Statement Respecting the New Catalogues of the College Library," *Report of the Committee of the Overseers of Harvard College Appointed To Visit the Library for the Year 1863: Together with the Accompaning Documents. Submitted January 28, 1864* (Boston: 1864), p.35.
27. Astor Library, *Alphabetical Index* . . . (1849), p.xx-xxii.
28. The forty largest libraries were determined from the listings in Charles C. Jewett, *Appendix to the Report of the Board of Regents of the Smithsonian Institution, Containing a Report on the Public Libraries, January 1, 1850*. The list of printed catalogues in Charles A. Cutter, "Library Catalogues," p.577-622, was used to establish the catalogues printed by these libraries.
29. American Antiquarian Society, *Proceedings* . . . *1850*, p.14.
30. Broadly classed catalogues were published, for example, by Harvard in 1790; Yale in 1791 and 1808; Baltimore Library Company in 1798, 1802, and 1809; Boston Athenaeum in 1809; Charleston Library Society in 1811; Library of Congress in 1812; New York Society Library in 1813; and the Redwood Library of Newport in 1816.

31. New York Society Library, *The Charter, Bye-Laws, and Names of the Members of the New-York Society Library: With a Catalogue of the Books...* (New York: Printed by T. & J. Swords, 1793), p.3.

32. Allegheny College Library, *Catalogus...* (1823), p.136.

33. Boston Athenaeum, *Catalogue of Books...* (Boston: Printed by William L. Lewis, 1827), unpaged "Advertisement" at the beginning of the catalogue.

34. Harvard University Library, *Catalogus bibliothecae Harvardianae Cantabrigiae Nov-Anglorum* (Boston: typis Thomae & Johannis Fleet, 1790).

35. Baltimore Library Company, *A Catalogue of the Books...* (Baltimore: Printed by Edes & Leakin, 1809). A few years later this same arrangement was employed in at least two more catalogues: Bowdoin College, *Catalogue of the Library...* (Brunswick, Maine: Printed by Joseph Griffin, 1821), and New York Mercantile Library Association, *Catalogue of the Books...* (New York: Printed by Hopkins & Morris, 1825).

36. American Philosophical Society, *Catalogue of the Library...* (Philadelphia: Printed by Joseph R. A. Skerrett, 1824), p.x.

37. Charleston Library Society, *A Catalogue of the Books...* (Charleston: Printed by A. E. Miller, 1826), p.vii.

38. Philadelphia Library Company, *A Catalogue of the Books...* (Philadelphia: Printed by Zachariah Poulson, 1789).

39. U.S. Library of Congress, *Catalogue of the Library of the United States...* (Washington: Printed by Jonathan Elliot, 1815).

40. Catalogues were prepared according to this plan, for example, by Pennsylvania University in 1829, the Library Company of Philadelphia in 1835, New York Mercantile Library in 1837, Loganian Library in 1837, Providence Athenaeum in 1837, Philadelphia Mercantile Library in 1840, and the Library of Congress in 1840.

41. Philadelphia Library Company, *A Catalogue of the Books...* (Philadelphia: Printed by Bartram & Reynolds, 1807).

42. Harvard University Library, *A Catalogue of the Library...* (3 vols.; Cambridge: E. W. Metcalf, 1830-31).

43. Jacques Charles Brunet, *Manuel du libraire et de l'amateur de livres...* (3 vols.; Paris: 1810).

44. Harvard University Library, *A Catalogue of the Library...* (1830), 3, Part I: v.

45. Andover Theological Seminary Library, *Catalogue of the Library...* (Andover, Mass.: Printed by Gould & Newman, 1838).

46. *Ibid.*, p.iii.

47. Charles C. Jewett, *Appendix to the Report of the Board of Regents of the Smithsonian Institution, Containing a Report on the Public Libraries, January 1, 1850*, p.19.

48. Andover Theological Seminary Library, *Catalogue of the Library...* (1838), p.vi.

49. Joseph A. Borome, *Charles Coffin Jewett* (Chicago: American Library Association, 1951), p.7.

50. Brown University Library, *A Catalogue of the Library... with an Index of Subjects* (Providence: 1843), p.xix.

51. *Ibid.*, p.xx.

52. The term, "subject-word entry," was widely employed by librarians during the nineteenth century and was defined by Cutter as an entry "made under a word of the title which indicates the subject of the book" (Charles A. Cutter, *Rules for a Printed Dictionary Catalogue* [Washington: Govt. Print. Off., 1876], p.14). The difference between the subject-word entries and the subject entries was, of course, that the latter were not limited to those words which the author chanced to include in the title.

53. Review of *A Catalogue of the Library of Brown University . . . North American Review*, 58:232 (Jan., 1844).
54. New York Mercantile Library, *Annual Report . . . 1844*, p.10.
55. Maysel O. Baker, "American Library Catalogs a Hundred Years Ago," *Wilson Library Bulletin*, 33:285 (Dec., 1958).
56. The manner in which the books were arranged on the library shelves was one of the items Jewett reported on in his *Appendix to the Report of the Board of Regents of the Smithsonian Institution, Containing a Report on the Public Libraries, January 1, 1850*.
57. Anthony Panizzi, "Rules for the Compilation of the Catalogue," British Museum, Department of Printed Books, *Catalogue of Printed Books in the British Museum*. Volume I (London: 1841), p.v-ix.
58. Allegheny College Library, *Catalogus . . .* (1823), p.136.
59. See Rules IX, XLVII, and LXXX in Panizzi, *op. cit.*, p.v, vii, ix.
60. American Philosophical Society, *Catalogue of the Library . . .* (1824), p.x.
61. See Rules LIV-LXVIII of Panizzi, *op. cit.*, p.vii-viii.
62. Harvard University Library, *A Catalogue of the Library . . .* (1830), 1:xvii.
63. Panizzi, *op. cit.*, p.v-ix.
64. Andover Theological Seminary Library, *Catalogue of the Library . . .* (1838), p.vi.
65. *Ibid.*, p.300.
66. New York Mercantile Library Association, *Systematic Catalogue of Books . . .* (1837), p.vi.
67. *Ibid.*, p.255.

III. THE AGE OF JEWETT, 1850-1875: GENERAL CONSIDERATIONS

1. Jesse Hauk Shera, *Foundations of the Public Library: The Origins of the Public Library Movement in New England, 1629-1855* (Chicago: Univ. of Chicago Pr., 1949), p.247.
2. Frederic B. Perkins, "Young Men's Mercantile Libraries," U.S. Bureau of Education, *Public Libraries in the United States . . .*, Special Report, Part I (Washington: Govt. Print. Off., 1876), p.380.
3. Henry A. Homes, "State and Territorial Libraries," U.S. Bureau of Education, *Public Libraries in the United States . . .*, Special Report, Part I (Washington: Govt. Print. Off., 1876), p.294-99.
4. —— "Historical Societies in the United States," *ibid.*, p.375-77.
5. Boston Public Library, *Index to the Catalogue of Books in the Upper Hall of the Public Library . . .* (Boston: G. C. Rand & Avery, 1861), p.iv.
6. Charles Coffin Jewett, *. . . On the Construction of Catalogues of Libraries, and Their Publication by Means of Separate, Stereotyped Titles, with Rules and Examples*, Smithsonian Report (2d ed.; Washington: Smithsonian Institution, 1853), p.15. Cited hereafter by title only.
7. Astor Library, *Catalogue or Alphabetical Index of the Astor Library: In Two Parts. Part 1, Authors and Books* (4 vols.; New York: R. Craighead, 1857-61), 1:iv.
8. Charles A. Cutter, "The Cataloguer's Work," *The Nation*, 24:87 (Feb. 8, 1877).
9. *Ibid.*
10. H. A. Hagen, "The Librarian's Work," *The Nation*, 24:40 (Jan. 18, 1877).
11. Cutter, *op. cit.*, p.87.
12. *Ibid.*
13. "The Proceedings ₁of the Philadelphia Conference of the American Library Association, 1876₁, Sixth Session," *Library Journal*, 1:131 (Nov., 1876).

14. Chicago Public Library, *Fifth Annual Report... 1877,* p.32.
15. Charles A. Cutter, "Library Catalogues," p.554-55.
16. Boston Public Library, *Twentieth Annual Report... 1872,* p.29-30.
17. Charles A. Cutter, "Library Catalogues," p.553.
18. New Bedford, Massachusetts, Public Library, *Seventh Annual Report... 1858,* p.9.
19. "The Proceedings ₍of the Philadelphia Conference of the American Library Association, 1876₎, Sixth Session," *Library Journal,* 1:130 (Nov., 1876).
20. P. L. Ford, review of *Public Libraries in America,* by W. I. Fletcher, *Library Journal,* 19:237-38 (July, 1894).
21. The information in this paragraph was drawn from the U.S. Bureau of Education, *Public Libraries in the United States ...,* Special Report, Part I. (Washington: Govt. Print. Off., 1876). The article on "Library Reports and Statistics," p.762-73, supplied the list of libraries with collections in excess of 20,000 volumes. Although these tables contain some inaccuracies and some omissions, it is not believed that they are such as significantly to alter the facts.
22. Catalogues of all, or of substantial portions, of their collections were printed by the state library of California in 1855, 1857, 1860, 1866, and 1870-71; Illinois in 1869 and 1871; Kentucky in 1872; Louisiana in 1869 and 1871; Maine in 1850 and 1856; Maryland in 1851 and 1874; Massachusetts in 1858; Michigan in 1850, 1857, 1861, 1870, 1873, and 1875; New York in 1850, 1855-56, and 1872; Ohio in 1875; Pennsylvania in 1853, 1859, and 1873; Virginia in 1856; and Wisconsin in 1852 and 1872.
23. Amherst College printed a catalogue in 1855, with a supplement in 1871; Bowdoin College in 1862; Columbia University in 1874; Dartmouth College in 1868; Marietta College in 1857; Ohio Wesleyan University in 1870; U.S. Military Academy at West Point in 1853—with a supplement in 1860—and in 1873; Williams College in 1852, 1861, and 1875; and the University of Georgia in 1850 and 1858.
24. Quincy, Massachusetts, Public Library, *Catalogue ...* (Boston: Rockwell & Churchill, 1875), p.1.
25. Examples are: Boston Public Library, *A Catalogue of Books Belonging to the Lower Hall of the Central Department, in the Classes of History, Biography, and Travel ... Together with Notes for Readers under Subject-References* (2d or consolidated ed.; Boston: 1873); Quincy, Massachusetts, Public Library, *Catalogue ...* (1875).
26. U.S. Library of Congress, *Alphabetical Catalogue of the Library of Congress: Authors* (Washington: Govt. Print. Off., 1864).
27. Boston Athenaeum, *Catalogue of the Library of the Boston Athenaeum, 1807-1871* (5 vols.; Boston: 1874-82).
28. Charles C. Jewett, *Appendix to the Report of the Board of Regents of the Smithsonian Institution, Containing a Report on the Public Libraries, January 1, 1850.*
29. "General Statistics of All Public Libraries in the United States," U.S. Bureau of Education, *Public Libraries in the United States ...,* Special Report, Part I (Washington: Govt. Print. Off., 1876), p.1010-1142.
30. *Ibid.*
31. U.S. Library of Congress, *Catalogue ...* (Washington: L. Towers, 1861).
32. —— *Alphabetical Catalogue... (1864).*
33. —— *Catalogue of the Library of Congress: Index of Subjects* (2 vols.; Washington: Govt. Print. Off., 1869).
34. A supplement was printed in this year which contained approximately 34,000 volumes: *Index to the Catalogue of Books in the Bates Hall of the Public Library of the City of Boston. First Supplement* (Boston: J. E. Farwell, 1866).

35. James L. Whitney, "Considerations as to a Printed Catalogue in Book Form," Boston Public Library, *Forty-Seventh Annual Report...1898*, p.52.
36. Weston Flint, *Statistics of Public Libraries in the United States and Canada* ("U.S. Bureau of Education, Circular of Information," No. 7, 1893 [Washington: Govt. Print. Off., 1893]), p.80.
37. San Francisco Mercantile Library Association, *Twenty-Second Annual Report...1874*, p.8.
38. Whitney, *op. cit.*, p.54.
39. Melvil Dewey, "The A.L.A. Catalog," *Library Journal*, 10:76 (Apr., 1885).
40. San Francisco Mercantile Library Association, *Twenty-Second Annual Report...1874*, p.8.
41. "General Statistics of All Public Libraries in the United States," U.S. Bureau of Education, *Public Libraries in the United States* ..., Special Report, Part I (Washington: Govt. Print. Off., 1876), p.1015.
42. *Ibid.*, p.1051.
43. Boston Public Library, *Twentieth Annual Report...1872*, p.29.
44. Charles A. Cutter, "Library Catalogues," p.552.
45. William F. Poole, "The Organization and Management of Public Libraries," U.S. Bureau of Education, *Public Libraries in the United States* ..., Special Report, Part I (Washington: Govt. Print. Off., 1876), p.497.
46. The information in this paragraph was taken from Charles A. Cutter, "Library Catalogues," p.568-71.
47. "The Proceedings [of the Philadelphia Conference of the American Library Association, 1876], Sixth Session," *Library Journal*, 1:131 (Nov., 1876).
48. Springfield, Massachusetts, City Library Association, *Annual Report...1872*, p.9.
49. Worcester, Massachusetts, Public Library, *Eleventh Annual Report...1871*, p.22.
50. San Francisco Mercantile Library Association, *Twenty-Second Annual Report...1874*, p.23.
51. *Ibid.*
52. Harvard University Library, *Continuatio supplementi Catalogi librorum Bibliothecae Collegij Harvardini* ... (Boston: B. Green, 1725); *Continuatio Catalogi librorum, Bibliothecae Collegij Harvardini: Ab anno 1725, ad annum 1735* [n.p.: n.d.].
53. Charles A. Cutter, "Library Catalogues," p.554.
54. Charles C. Jewett, ...*On the Construction of Catalogues* ..., p.7.
55. *Ibid.*, p.29-64.
56. *Ibid.*, p.9.
57. *Ibid.*, p.ix.
58. *Ibid.*, p.xi.
59. George Burwell Utley, *The Librarians' Conference of 1853: A Chapter in American Library History*, ed. Gilbert H. Doane (Chicago: American Library Association, 1951), p.151.
60. American Antiquarian Society, *Proceedings...1855*, p.30-32.
61. Boston Public Library, *Catalogue of the Public Library of the City of Boston* ... (Boston: J. Wilson & Son, 1854).
62. Boston Mercantile Library Association, *Catalogue* ... (Boston: John Wilson & Son, 1854).
63. Boston Public Library, *Second Annual Report...1854*, p.12-13.
64. Boston Mercantile Library Association, *Thirty-Fifth Annual Report...1855*, p.30-31.
65. Cincinnati Young Men's Mercantile Library Association, *Catalogue* ... (Cincinnati: Truman & Spofford, 1855); Philadelphia Mercantile Library Company, *Catalogue of Books Added...since April, 1850* (Philadelphia: T. K. &

P. G. Collins, 1856); Brooklyn Mercantile Library Association, *A Catalogue of Books* ... (Brooklyn: Baker & Godwin, 1858); New Bedford, Massachusetts, Free Public Library, *Catalogue* ... (New Bedford: B. Lindsey, 1858).

66. New York Mercantile Library, *Catalogue* ... (New York: Edward O. Jenkins, 1844).

67. Astor Library, *Annual Report of the Trustees* ... *1854*, p.30.

68. —— *Catalogue of Books* ... *Relating to the Languages and Literature of Asia, Africa, and the Oceanic Islands* (New York: Astor Library Autographic Pr., 1854).

69. Boston Public Library, ... *Finding List for Alcoves IV and VII* ₗ*Fiction*₁ (Boston: 1866); *Finding List* ... *History, Politics, etc.* (Boston: 1866); ... *Finding List* ... *Containing Works in the Sciences, Arts and Professions* ... (Boston: 1866); ... *Finding List* ... *French, German and Italian Books* (Boston: 1867); ... *Finding List* ... *Biography and Travels* (Boston, 1868); ... *Class List for Poetry, the Drama, Rhetoric, Elocution, Collections, Periodicals, and Miscellaneous Works* (Boston: 1870).

70. —— *Fifteenth Annual Report* ... *1867*, p.9-10.

71. —— *Bulletin*, Vols. 1-14 (Oct., 1867 - Jan., 1896).

72. —— *Sixteenth Annual Report* ... *1868*, p.72.

73. *The Athenaeum Centenary: The Influence and History of the Boston Athenaeum from 1807 to 1907* ... (Boston: Boston Athenaeum, 1907), p.93.

74. Charles A. Cutter, "Library Catalogues," p.575.

75. Cincinnati Public Library, *Sixth Annual Report* ... *1873*, p.23.

76. Astor Library, *Annual Report* ... *1854*, p.30.

77. Quoted in "The Astor Library," *Library Journal*, 6:259 (Sept.-Oct., 1881).

78. Maysel O. Baker, "American Library Catalogs a Hundred Years Ago," *Wilson Library Bulletin*, 33:284 (Dec., 1958).

79. Ezra Abbot, " ... Statement Respecting the New Catalogues of the College Library," Harvard University, *Report of the Committee of the Overseers of Harvard College Appointed To Visit the Library for the Year 1863* ... (Boston: 1864), p.43.

80. Boston Public Library, *Twentieth Annual Report* ... *1872*, p.28.

81. St. Louis, Missouri, Public School Library, *Annual Report* ... *1871/72*, p.12.

82. Charles A. Cutter, "Library Catalogues," p.555.

83. Otis H. Robinson, "College Library Administration," U.S. Bureau of Education, *Public Libraries in the United States* ... , Special Report, Part I (Washington: Govt. Print. Off., 1876), p.512.

IV. THE AGE OF JEWETT, 1850-1875: CATALOGUE ARRANGEMENT

1. See p.23.

2. Boston Athenaeum, *Catalogue* ... (Boston: 1810).

3. Charleston Library Society, *A Catalogue of Books* ... *January, 1811* (Charleston: Printed by W. P. Young, 1811).

4. U.S. Library of Congress, *Catalogue of the Books, Maps, and Charts* ... (Washington: Printed by Roger C. Weightman, 1812).

5. Yale University Library, *Catalogue of Books* ... (New Haven, Conn.: Printed by T. & S. Green, 1791).

6. University of Pennsylvania Library, *Catalogue of Books* ... (Philadelphia: J. Dobson, 1829).

7. Library Company of Philadelphia, *A Catalogue of the Books* ... (2 vols.; Philadelphia: C. Sherman, 1835).

8. New York Society Library, *Alphabetical and Analytical Catalogue* ... (New York: Printed by James Van Norden, 1838).

9. Brown University Library, *A Catalogue of the Library* ... (1843), p.xx.
10. Charles A. Cutter, "Library Catalogues," p.529.
11. William T. Harris, "Essay on the System of Classification," St. Louis, Missouri, Public School Library, *Catalogue, Classified and Alphabetical, of the Books* ... (St. Louis: Missouri Democrat Book and Job Print. House, 1870), p.x.
12. Philadelphia Mercantile Library Company, *A Catalogue ... Published April, 1850* (Philadelphia: 1850).
13. *Ibid.*, p.x.
14. New York Society Library, *Alphabetical and Analytical Catalogue* ... (New York: R. Craighead, 1850).
15. Charles A. Cutter, "Library Catalogues," p.532.
16. New York Mercantile Library Association, *Catalogue of Books ... with a Supplement to August 1, 1856* (New York: Baker & Godwin, 1856); Peabody Institute, Baltimore, Library, *Alphabetical Catalogue of Books Proposed To Be Purchased* ... (Baltimore: Printed by J. D. Toy, 1861).
17. General Society of Mechanics and Tradesmen of the City of New York, Library, *Catalogue of the Apprentices' Library in New-York. Established and Supported by the General Society of Mechanics and Tradesmen. September, 1865* (New York: A. W. King, 1865).
18. New York Mercantile Library Association, *Catalogue of Books* ... (New York: F. T. Taylor, 1866).
19. Melvil Dewey, "A Decimal Classification and Subject Index," U.S. Bureau of Education, *Public Libraries in the United States* ..., Special Report, Part I (Washington: Govt. Print. Off., 1876), p.636.
20. Charles Coffin Jewett, ... *On the Construction of Catalogues* ..., p.7.
21. Boston Public Library, *Index to the Catalogue of a Portion of the Public Library of the City of Boston, Arranged in the Lower Hall* ... (Boston: G. C. Rand & Avery, 1858); *Index to the Catalogue of Books in the Upper Hall* ... (1861).
22. Silas Bronson Library, Waterbury, Connecticut, *Catalogue* ... (Waterbury, Conn.: American Print. Co., 1870).
23. Cincinnati Public Library, *Catalogue* ... (Cincinnati: Wilstach, Baldwin & Co., 1871).
24. William F. Poole, "The Organization and Management of Public Libraries," U.S. Bureau of Education, *Public Libraries in the United States* ..., Special Report, Part I (Washington: Govt. Print. Off., 1876), p.498.
25. Cambridge, Massachusetts, High School Library, *A Classed Catalogue of the Library* ... (Cambridge, Mass.: John Bartlett, 1853).
26. Ezra Abbot, "... Statement Respecting the New Catalogues of the College Library," Harvard University, *Report of the Committee of the Overseers of Harvard College Appointed To Visit the Library for the Year 1863* ... (Boston: 1864), p.47.
27. *Ibid.*, p.46.
28. Astor Library, *Annual Report ... 1854*, p.30.
29. —— *Catalogue or Alphabetical Index ... In Two Parts. Part I, Authors and Books* (4 vols.; New York: R. Craighead, 1857-61).
30. *Ibid.*, p.v.
31. Charles A. Cutter, "Library Catalogues," p.531.
32. *Ibid.*, p.532.
33. —— *Expansive Classification, Part I: The First Six Classifications* (Boston: C. A. Cutter, 1891-93).
34. —— *Rules for a Printed Dictionary Catalogue* (Washington: Govt. Print. Off., 1876).

35. Dewey, *op. cit.*, p.635.
36. —— *A Classification and Subject Index for Cataloguing and Arranging the Books and Pamphlets of a Library* (Amherst, Mass.: 1876). The term, "Relativ Index," appears in the titles of all later editions except the Standard (15th) edition published in 1951.
37. Charles A. Cutter, "The Athenaeum Catalogue," *Library Journal,* 3:191-92 (July, 1878).
38. —— "Library Catalogues," p.534.
39. Boston Mercantile Library Association, *A Catalogue of Books* ... (Boston: Printed by Freeman & Bolles, 1844).
40. William F. Poole, *An Alphabetical Index to Subjects, Treated in the Reviews, and Other Periodicals* ... (New York: Putnam, 1848); *An Index to Periodical Literature* (New York: C. B. Norton, 1853).
41. Boston Mercantile Library Association, *Catalogue* ... (Boston: John Wilson & Son, 1854), p.v-vi.
42. *Ibid.*, p.vi.
43. William F. Poole, "The Plan of the New 'Poole's Index,'" *Library Journal,* 3:110 (May, 1878).
44. Boston Mercantile Library Association, *Catalogue* ... (1854); Cincinnati Public Library, *Catalogue* ... (1871); Chicago Public Library, *Temporary Finding Lists for Alcoves A. to L., July, 1874* (1874).
45. Charles A. Cutter, "The Editor to the Proprietors," Boston Athenaeum, *Catalogue of the Library* ... *1807-1871* (Boston: 1874-82), 5:3399.
46. Charles Coffin Jewett, ... *On the Construction of Catalogues* ... , p.14-16.
47. Boston Public Library, *Sixth Annual Report* ... *1858,* p.29.
48. —— *Index to the Catalogue of a Portion of the Public Library of the City of Boston, Arranged in the Lower Hall* (1858), p.iii.
49. —— *Sixth Annual Report* ... *1858,* p.30.
50. *Ibid.*
51. Abbot, *op. cit.,* p.45-46.
52. Joseph A. Borome, *Charles Coffin Jewett* (Chicago: American Library Association, 1951), p.123-29.
53. Philadelphia Mercantile Library Company, *Catalogue* ... (Philadelphia: 1870); Buffalo Young Men's Association Library, *Catalogue* ... (Buffalo: 1871).
54. Abbot, *op. cit.,* p.35.
55. *Ibid.,* p.48.
56. *Ibid.,* p.47.
57. *Ibid.,* p.55.
58. *Ibid.,* p.50.
59. Charles A. Cutter, "The New Catalogue of Harvard College Library," *North American Review,* 108:107 (Jan., 1869).
60. Abbot, *op. cit.,* p.59.
61. Charles A. Cutter, "The Editor to the Proprietors," Boston Athenaeum, *Catalogue of the Library* ... *1807-1871* (Boston: 1874-82), 5:3399-3400.
62. —— "The New Catalogue of Harvard College Library," *North American Review,* 108:96-129 (Jan., 1869).
63. —— "Library Catalogues," p.540.
64. From a statement by Justin Winsor in "The Plan of the New 'Poole's Index': A Library Symposium," *Library Journal,* 3:143 (June, 1878).
65. Jacob Schwartz, "New York Apprentices' Library Catalogue," U.S. Bureau of Education, *Public Libraries in the United States* ..., Special Report, Part I (Washington: Govt. Print. Off., 1876), p.659.
66. *Ibid.,* p.660.

V. THE DECLINE OF THE PRINTED BOOK CATALOGUE

1. Figures are based upon two publications of the U.S. Bureau of Education.
   The statistics of library holdings at the beginning of the final quarter of
   the nineteenth century were taken from "Library Reports and Statistics,"
   Public Libraries in the United States ..., Special Report, Part I (Washington: Govt. Print. Off., 1876), p.762-73; the statistics for libraries at the
   end of the century were taken from the *Report of the Commissioner of Education for the Year 1899-1900* (Washington: Govt. Print. Off., 1901),
   1:923-1165.
2. William I. Fletcher, "Annotation," *Library Journal*, 29:144 (St. Louis Conference Number, 1904).
3. —— *Public Libraries in America* (Boston: Roberts Bros., 1894), p.57.
4. *Ibid.*, p.58.
5. Frederick M. Crunden, "Report on Aids and Guides," *Library Journal*,
   11:309 (Milwaukee Conference Number, 1886).
6. William C. Lane, "Cataloging," *Papers Prepared for the World's Library
   Congress Held at the Columbian Exposition*, ed. Melvil Dewey (Washington:
   Govt. Print. Off., 1896), p.835-49.
7. *Ibid.*, p.838.
8. Libraries with collections in excess of 100,000 volumes were determined
   from listings in U.S. Bureau of Education, *Report of the Commissioner of
   Education for the Year 1899-1900* (Washington: Govt. Print. Off., 1901),
   1:923-1165.
9. U.S. Surgeon-General's Office, *Index-Catalogue of the Library of the
   Surgeon-General's Office, United States Army: Authors and Subjects* ...
   (16 vols.; Washington: Govt. Print. Off., 1880-95).
10. —— *Index-Catalogue of the Library of the Surgeon-General's Office* (Wash-
    ington: Govt. Print. Off., 1896-1948). Ceased publication in 1948 with Vol-
    ume 10 of Series 4.
11. Peabody Institute, Baltimore, Library, *Catalogue* ... (5 vols.; Baltimore:
    1883-92).
12. —— —— *Second Catalogue* ... *Including the Additions Made since 1882*
    (8 vols.; Baltimore: 1896-1905).
13. U.S. Surgeon-General's Office, *Index-Catalogue* ... (1880-95), 1:iii.
14. Peabody Institute, Baltimore, Library, *Catalogue* ... (1883-92), 1:iii.
15. From an unsigned editorial, presumably by Charles A. Cutter, the editor,
    Library Journal, 8:335 (Dec., 1883).
16. George E. Wire, review of *Index-Catalogue of the Library of the Surgeon-
    General's Office*, *Library Journal*, 20:395 (Nov., 1895).
17. James L. Whitney, "Considerations as to a Printed Catalogue in Book
    Form," Boston Public Library, *Forty-Seventh Annual Report* ... *1898*, p.54.
18. Massachusetts State Library, *Catalogue* ... (Boston: Rand, Avery & Co.,
    1880).
19. Cleveland Public Library, *Alphabetic Catalogue of the English Books in the
    Circulating Department of the Cleveland Public Library: Authors, Titles
    and Subjects. 1889* (Cleveland: Cleveland Print. & Pub. Co., 1889).
20. Brooklyn Library, *Catalogue of the Mercantile Library of Brooklyn: Au-
    thors, Titles, Subjects, and Classes* (3 vols.; Brooklyn: 1877-80).
21. Stephen B. Noyes, "Cataloguing," *Library Journal*, 8:168 (Buffalo Confer-
    ence Number, 1883).
22. Brooklyn Library, *Catalogue of the Mercantile Library of Brooklyn: Au-
    thors, Titles, Subjects, and Classes* (3 vols.: Brooklyn, 1877-80), 1: un-
    paged Preface.
23. Stephen B. Noyes, "Plan of New Catalogue of the Brooklyn Mercantile Li-

brary," U.S. Bureau of Education, *Public Libraries in the United States...* Special Report, Part I (Washington: Govt. Print. Off., 1876), p.649.

24. Charles A. Cutter, "Library Catalogues," p.545.

25. *Ibid.*

26. Justin Winsor, "The President's Address: Conference of Librarians, Washington, February, 1881," *Library Journal,* 6:64 (Washington Conference Number, 1881).

27. Haverhill, Massachusetts, Public Library, *Catalogue...* (Haverhill: Press of Franklin P. Stiles, 1878).

28. Fall River, Massachusetts, Public Library, *Catalogue...* (Fall River: Press of Fiske & Munroe, 1882).

29. Melvil Dewey, "A Decimal Classification and Subject Index," U.S. Bureau of Education, *Public Libraries in the United States...*, Special Report, Part I (Washington: Govt. Print. Off., 1876), p.635.

30. *Ibid.*

31. —— *A Classification and Subject Index for Cataloguing and Arranging the Books and Pamphlets of a Library* (Amherst, Mass.: 1876).

32. *A.L.A. Catalog: 8,000 Volumes for a Popular Library, with Notes...*, ed. Melvil Dewey (Washington: Govt. Print. Off., 1904).

33. Arthur Goldberg, *The Buffalo Public Library: Commemorating Its First Century of Service to the Citizens of Buffalo, 1836-1936* (Buffalo: Privately printed, 1937).

34. Milwaukee Public Library, *Third Annual Report for the Year Ending August 31, 1880* (Milwaukee: The Library, 1880), p.21.

35. —— *Systematic Catalogue of the Public Library of the City of Milwaukee: With Alphabetical Author, Title, and Subject Indexes. 1885* (Milwaukee: Board of Trustees, 1885-86).

36. William C. Lane, "Report on Catalogues and Aids and Guides for Readers, 1885-87," *Library Journal,* 12:415-16 (Thousand Islands Conference Number, 1887).

37. Fitchburg, Massachusetts, Public Library, *Classified Catalogue of the Public Library, of Fitchburg, Mass.: Comprising Author and Title Catalogue, Subject Catalogue, and Subject Index,* comp. George Watson Cole (Fitchburg: Press of Blanchard & Brown, 1886).

38. Pittsburgh Carnegie Library, *Classified Catalogue of the Carnegie Library of Pittsburgh, 1895-1902...* (Pittsburgh: Carnegie Library, 1907).

39. William Warner Bishop, "Margaret Mann," *Catalogers' and Classifiers' Yearbook,* 7:11-12 (1938).

40. "[Proceedings of the] Conference of Librarians, Catskills, Sept. 25-28, 1888... Third Day—Thursday, September 27," *Library Journal,* 13:315 (Catskills Conference Number, 1888).

41. *Ibid.*

42. Whitney, *op. cit.,* p.49-59.

43. Charles Coffin Jewett,... *On the Construction of Catalogues of Libraries...*, p.1-28.

44. Willi Mengel, *Ottmar Mergenthaler and the Printing Revolution: With an Introduction by Lin Yutang* (Brooklyn: Mergenthaler Linotype Co., 1954), p.50-57.

45. *Ibid.,* p.53.

46. Ernest C. Richardson, "The Linotype Method," *Library Journal,* 17:377 (Sept., 1892).

47. *Ibid.*

48. "[Proceedings of the] Conference of Librarians, Lakewood, N.J., Baltimore, Washington, May 16-21, 1892," *Library Journal,* 17:28-29 (Lakewood Conference Number, 1892).

49. Enoch Pratt Free Library, Baltimore, *Finding List... July, 1893* (3 vols.; 5th ed.; Baltimore: Friedenwald Co., 1893-94).

50. Northampton, Massachusetts, Forbes Library, *First Annual Report for Year Ending November 30, 1895*, p.10.

51. From a statement by Willis K. Stetson, Librarian, Free Public Library, New Haven, Connecticut, in "Linotyping Library Catalogs: A Symposium," *Library Journal*, 19:259 (Aug., 1894).

52. Nathan Billstein, "Linotyping Library Catalogs—Pro and Con," *Library Journal*, 19:258 (Aug., 1894).

53. Whitney, *op. cit.*, p.56.

54. Alexander J. Rudolph, "The Blue-Print Process for Printing Catalogs," *Library Journal*, 24:102 (Mar., 1899).

55. *Ibid.*, 104-5.

56. British Museum, Department of Printed Books, *Catalogue of Printed Books in the Library of the British Museum* ... (95 vols.; London: Printed by W. Clowes & Sons, 1881-1900).

57. "The Newberry Blue-Print Catalog," *Library Journal*, 24:574 (Oct., 1899).

58. Charles Martel, "The Newberry Blue-Print Catalog," *Library Journal*, 24:608 (Nov., 1899).

59. From an unsigned editorial in the *Library Journal*, 24:560 (Oct., 1899).

60. "[Proceedings of the] Conference of Librarians, San Francisco, October 12-16, 1891 ... Eighth Session," *Library Journal*, 16:121 (San Francisco Conference Number, 1891).

61. *Ibid.*

62. "[Proceedings of the] Conference of Librarians, Lakewood, N.J., Baltimore, Washington, May 16-21, 1892 ... First Session," *Library Journal*, 17:23 (Lakewood Conference Number, 1892).

63. From an unsigned editorial in the *Library Journal*, 18:277 (Aug., 1893).

64. William C. Lane, "Cataloging," *Papers Prepared for the World's Library Congress Held at the Columbian Exposition*, ed. Melvil Dewey (Washington: Govt. Print. Off., 1896), p.839.

65. George E. Wire, "Report on Classification and Cataloging," *Library Journal*, 23:20 (Chautauqua Conference Number, 1898).

66. Chicago Public Library, *Temporary Finding Lists for Alcoves A. to L., July, 1874* (1874).

67. —— *First Annual Report... 1873*, p.26.

68. —— *Temporary Finding Lists, February, 1875* (2d ed.; Chicago: Hazlitt & Reed, 1875); *Finding Lists* ... (3d ed.; Chicago: Printed by Jefferson & Wroe, 1876).

69. —— *Fifth Annual Report... 1877*, p.33.

70. *Ibid.*, p.32.

71. —— *Thirteenth Annual Report... 1885*, p.24.

72. Minneapolis Public Library, *Finding List: Part III, February, 1890* (Minneapolis: Tribune Job Print. Co., 1890); Bloomington, Illinois, Withers Public Library, *Finding List, November, 1894* (Bloomington: J. E. Burke & Co., 1894); Decatur, Illinois, Public Library, *Catalogue* ... (Decatur: Herald-Despatch Co., 1894).

73. Providence, Rhode Island, Public Library, *Finding List... 1880* (Providence: E. L. Freeman, 1880).

74. Galesburg, Illinois, Public Library, *Finding List... 1887* (Galesburg: Press of Colville & Bro., 1887); Los Angeles Public Library, *Finding List... January, 1891* (Los Angeles: Times-Mirror Print. and Bind. House, 1891).

75. Jersey City, New Jersey, Public Library, *Alphabetical Finding List... August 1, 1891* (Jersey City: Jersey City Print. Co., 1891).

76. Utica, New York, Public Library, *Finding List, May, 1895* (Utica: L. C. Childs & Son, 1895).

77. William I. Fletcher, *Public Libraries in America* (Boston: Roberts Bros., 1894), p.57.

78. George E. Wire, "Report on Classification and Cataloging," *Library Journal*, 23:21 (Chautauqua Conference Number, 1898).

79. "American Library Association," *Library Journal*, 1:252-53 (Mar., 1877).

80. Charles A. Nelson, "Publishers' Slips for Librarians and Others," *Library Journal*, 1:15 (Sept., 1876).

81. Melvil Dewey, "Public Documents," *Library Journal*, 1:11 (Sept., 1876).

82. ———— "The Coming Catalogue," *Library Journal*, 1:423-27 (Aug., 1877).

83. "The Proceedings [of the Conference of Librarians, Philadelphia, October 4-6, 1876], Fourth Session," *Library Journal*, 1:116-17 (Nov., 1876).

84. *Ibid.*, p.118.

85. William I. Fletcher, "The Future of the Catalog," *Library Journal*, 30:143 (Mar., 1905).

86. "Proceedings of the Conference of Librarians, Milwaukee Meeting, July 7-10, 1886 ... Appendix I, The Publishing Section," *Library Journal*, 11:382 (Milwaukee Conference Number, 1886).

87. The first edition was published under the title *An Alphabetical Index to Subjects, Treated in the Reviews, and Other Periodicals ...* (New York: Putnam, 1848).

88. The notable exceptions, of course, were the 1874-82 catalogue of the Boston Athenaeum; the 1875 catalogue of the Quincy, Massachusetts, Public Library; the 1877-80 catalogue of the Brooklyn Library; and the 1883-92 and 1896-1905 catalogues of the Peabody Institute Library of Baltimore.

89. The title of the second edition was *An Index to Periodical Literature* (New York: C. B. Norton, 1853).

90. "The Proceedings [of the Conference of Librarians, Philadelphia, October 4-6, 1876], Fourth Session," *Library Journal*, 1:116-17 (Nov., 1876).

91. William F. Poole, *An Index to Periodical Literature: Brought down to Jan. 1882 with the Assistance as Associate Editor of William I. Fletcher ... and the Cooperation of the American Library Association and the Library Association of the United Kingdom ...* (3d ed.; Boston: J. R. Osgood & Co., 1882).

92. "[Proceedings of the] Conference of Librarians, Cincinnati, May, 1882 ... First Session," *Library Journal*, 7:194 (Cincinnati Conference Number, 1882).

93. *"A.L.A." Index ...* (Boston: Houghton, 1893).

94. "The Proceedings [of the Conference of Librarians, New York, September, 1877], Fourth Session," *Library Journal*, 2:34 (New York Conference Number, 1877).

95. Samuel S. Green, "Report of the Committee on the Distribution of Public Documents," *Library Journal*, 6:89 (Washington Conference Number, 1881).

96. Melvil Dewey, "The Coming Catalogue," *Library Journal*, 1:423-27 (Aug., 1877).

97. "A.L.A. Catalog," *Library Journal*, 4:123 (Apr., 1879).

98. *Catalog of "A.L.A." Library: 5,000 Volumes for a Popular Library, Selected by the American Library Association and Shown at the World's Columbian Exposition* (Washington: Govt. Print. Off., 1893).

99. Melvil Dewey, "The Coming Catalogue," *Library Journal*, 1:423 (Aug., 1877).

100. "The Proceedings [of the Conference of Librarians, Philadelphia, October 4-6, 1876], Fourth Session," *Library Journal*, 3:113-15 (May, 1878).

101. Melvil Dewey, "The Coming Catalogue," *Library Journal*, 1:423 (Aug., 1877).

102. "Report of Committee on Title-Slips," *Library Journal*, 3:113-115 (May, 1878).
103. "₍Proceedings of the₎ Conference of Librarians, Boston, June-July, 1879... Third Session," *Library Journal*, 4:291 (Boston Conference Number, 1879).
104. "Publisher's Note," *Library Journal*, 5:58 (Feb., 1880).
105. "Publication Section: Printed Catalog Cards," *Library Journal*, 12:515 (Nov., 1887).
106. "Central Card Cataloging," *Library Journal*, 18:508-10 (Dec., 1893).
107. William C. Lane, "Report of the A.L.A. Publishing Section," *Library Journal*, 22:84-86 (Philadelphia Conference Number, 1897).
108. Ernest C. Richardson, "Report of the Co-operation Committee," *Library Journal*, 25:72 (Montreal Conference Number, 1900).

Selected Bibliography

SELECTED LIBRARY CATALOGUES

During the course of this study some 1,000 library catalogues were examined. The great majority of them were rather poorly done, exhibited few innovations in cataloguing technique, and were frank imitations of the leading library catalogues of the day. Listed below in chronological order are 179 selected catalogues which, collectively, embody most of the significant developments in printed book catalogues prior to the end of the nineteenth century. These catalogues, for the most part, are also well executed and list the holdings of noteworthy collections.

Harvard University. Library. *Catalogus librorum Bibliothecae Collegij Harvardini quod est Cantabrigiae in Nova Anglia.* Bostoni Nov-Anglorum: typis B. Green, 1723.

Philadelphia. Library Company. *A Catalogue of Books Belonging to the Library Company of Philadelphia.* Philadelphia: Printed by B. Franklin, 1741.

Yale University. Library. *A Catalogue of the Library of Yale-College in New Haven.* N. London: Printed by T. Groen [sic], 1743. [New Haven: 1931].

Charleston Library Society, Charleston, S.C. *A Catalogue of the Books Belonging to the Charles-Town Library Society, in Charles-Town, South-Carolina.* London: Printed by W. Strahan for the Society, 1750.

Yale University. Library. *A Catalogue of Books in the Library of Yale-College in New-Haven.* New-Haven: Printed by James Parker, 1755.

Philadelphia. Library Company. *The Charter, Laws, and Catalogue*

of Books, of the Library Company of Philadelphia. Philadelphia: Printed by B. Franklin & D. Hall, 1757.
New York Society Library. *A Catalogue of the Books Belonging to
the New-York Society Library.* New York: Printed and Sold
by H. Gaine ₍1758₎.
Loganian Library, Philadelphia. *Catalogus Bibliothecae Loganianae.* . . . Philadelphia: Printed by Peter Miller & Comp.,
1760.
Princeton University. Library. *A Catalogue of Books in the Library of the College of New Jersey, January 29, 1760. Pub.
by Order of the Trustees at Woodbridge, New Jersey by
James Parker, 1760.* ₍Princeton₎: Reprinted by the Friends
of the Library, 1949.
New York Society Library. *A Catalogue of the Books Belonging to
the New-York Society Library.* New York: Printed by H.
Gaine, ₍1761₎.
Philadelphia. Library Company. *The Charter, Laws, and Catalogue of Books, of the Library Company of Philadelphia.* . . .
Philadelphia: Printed by B. Franklin & D. Hall, 1764.
Redwood Library and Athenaeum, Newport, R.I. *A Catalogue of
the Books Belonging to the Company of the Redwood-Library,
in Newport, on Rhode-Island.* Newport: Printed by S. Hall,
1764.
Philadelphia. Association Library Company. *A Catalogue of
Books, Belonging to the Association Library Company of
Philadelphia: Alphabetically Digested. To Which Is Prefixed,
the Articles of the Said Company, etc.* Philadelphia: Printed
by William Bradford, 1765.
Charleston Library Society, Charleston, S.C. *A Catalogue of
Books, Belonging to the Incorporated Charlestown Library So-
ciety, with the Dates of Editions.* . . . Charlestown: Printed for
the Society by R. Wells, 1770.
Philadelphia. Library Company. *The Charter, Laws, and Cata-
logue of Books, of the Library Company of Philadelphia. With
a Short Account of the Library Prefixed.* . . . Philadelphia:
Printed by Joseph Crukshank, 1770.
Charleston Library Society, Charleston, S.C. *A Catalogue of
Books, Given and Devised by John Mackenzie . . . to the
Charlestown Library Society, for the Use of the College When
Erected.* Charlestown: Printed for the Society by R. Wells,
1772.
Harvard University. Library. *Catalogus librorum in Bibliotheca
cantabrigiensi selectus, frequentiorem in usum Harvardina-
tum, qui gradu baccalaurei in artibus nondum sunt donati.*
Bostoniae, Nov. Ang.: Edes & Gill, 1773.

New York Society Library. *The Charter, and Bye-Laws, of the New-York Society Library: With a Catalogue of the Books Belonging to the Said Library.* New York: Printed by H. Gaine, 1773.

Philadelphia. Library Company. *A Catalogue of the Books, Belonging to the Library Company of Philadelphia: To Which Is Prefixed, a Short Account of the Institution, with the Charter, Laws and Regulations.* Philadelphia: Printed by Zachariah Poulson, 1789.

Harvard University. Library. *Catalogus bibliothecae Harvardianae Cantabrigiae Nov-Anglorum.* Bostoniae: typis Thomae et Johannis Fleet, 1790.

Yale University. Library. *Catalogue of Books in the Library of Yale-College, New Haven.* ₍New Haven₎: Printed by T. & S. Green, 1791.

Brown University. Library. *Catalogue of Books Belonging to the Library of Rhode-Island College.* Providence: Printed by J. Carter, 1793.

New York Society Library. *The Charter, Bye-Laws, and Names of the Members of the New-York Society Library: With a Catalogue of the Books Belonging to the Said Library.* New-York: Printed by T. & J. Swords, 1793.

Williams College. Library. *A Catalogue of Books in the Library of Williams College, Williamstown.* Bennington, ₍Vt.₎: Printed by Anthony Haswell, 1794.

Boston Library Society. *Catalogue of Books in the Boston Library. January 1, 1795.* ₍n.p., n.d.₎

Philadelphia. Library Company. Loganian Library. *Catalogue of the Books Belonging to the Loganian Library....* 2 vols. Philadelphia: Printed by Zachariah Poulson, 1795-1829.

Massachusetts Historical Society. Library. *Catalogue of Books in the Massachusetts Historical Library.* Boston: Printed by S. Hall, 1796.

Baltimore. Library Company. *A Catalogue of the Books, etc. Belonging to the Library Company of Baltimore: To Which Are Prefixed the Act for the Incorporation of the Company, Their Constitution, Their Bye-Laws, and an Alphabetical List of the Members.* Baltimore: Printed by John Hayes, 1798.

_____ _____ *A Catalogue of the Books, etc. Belonging to the Library Company of Baltimore; To Which Are Prefixed, the Act for the Incorporation of the Company, Their Constitution, Their By-Laws, and an Alphabetical List of the Members.* Baltimore: Printed by Prentiss & Cole, 1802.

U.S. Library of Congress. *Catalogue of Books, Maps, and Charts, Belonging to the Library of the Two Houses of Congress,*

April, 1802. Washington City: Printed by William Duane, [1802].

Boston Library Society. *Catalogue of Books in the Boston Library. Nov. 1, 1807.* [n.p., n.d.]

Philadelphia. Library Company. *A Catalogue of the Books, Belonging to the Library Company of Philadelphia: To Which Is Prefixed, a Short Account of the Institution, with the Charter, Laws, and Regulations.* Philadelphia: Printed by Bartram & Reynolds, 1807.

South Carolina. University. *Catalogue of Books Belonging to the South-Carolina College Library.* [n.p.]: Printed by Daniel & J. J. Faust, 1807.

Yale University. Library. *Catalogue of Books in the Library of Yale-College, New-Haven, January 1 ... January, 1808.* New-Haven: Printed by Oliver Steele & Co., 1808.

Baltimore. Library Company. *A Catalogue of the Books, etc. Belonging to the Library Company of Baltimore: To Which Are Prefixed the Act for the Incorporation of the Company, Their Constitution, Their By-Laws, and an Alphabetical List of the Members.* Baltimore: Printed by Edes & Leakin, 1809.

Charleston Library Society, Charleston, S.C. *A Catalogue of Books Belonging to the Charleston Library Society, January, 1811.* Charleston: Printed by W. P. Young, 1811.

U.S. Library of Congress. *Catalogue of the Books, Maps, and Charts, Belonging to the Library Established in the Capitol at the City of Washington, for the Two Houses of Congress: To Which Are Annexed the Statutes and Bye-Laws Relative to That Institution.* Washington City: Printed by Roger C. Weightman, 1812.

New York Historical Society. *Catalogue of the Books, Tracts, Newspapers, Maps, Charts, Views, Portraits, and Manuscripts, in the Library of the New-York Historical Society.* New-York: From the Press of J. Seymour, 1813.

New York Society Library. *A Catalogue of the Books Belonging to the New-York Society Library: Together with the Charter and By-Laws of the Same.* New-York: Printed by C. S. Van Winkle, 1813.

U.S. Library of Congress. *Catalogue of the Library of the United States: To Which Is Annexed, a Copious Index, Alphabetically Arranged.* Washington: Printed by Jonathan Elliot, 1815.

Redwood Library and Athenaeum, Newport, R.I. "Catalogue of the Books Belonging to the Redwood Library Company, in Newport, State of Rhode-Island, April, A.D. 1816," *Charter of the Redwood Library Company, Granted A.D. 1747,* p. 15-36. Newport: Printed by Rousmaniere & Barber, 1816.

Bowdoin College. Library. *Catalogue of the Library of Bowdoin College, in Brunswick, Maine.* Brunswick: Printed by Joseph Griffin, 1821.

Allegheny College, Meadville, Pa. Library. *Catalogus bibliothecae collegii Alleghaniensis.* Meadville: e typis Thomae Atkinson et Soc., 1823.

Yale University. Library. *Catalogue of Books in the Library of Yale College.* New Haven: Printed at the Journal Office, 1823.

American Philosophical Society. Library. *Catalogue of the Library of the American Philosophical Society, Held at Philadelphia, for Promoting Useful Knowledge. Published by Order of the Society.* Philadelphia: Printed by Joseph R. A. Skerrett, 1824.

New York. Mercantile Library Association. *Catalogue of the Books Belonging to the Mercantile Library Association of the City of New-York: To Which Are Prefixed, the Constitution and the Rules and Regulations of the Same.* New-York: Printed by Hopkins & Morris, 1825.

Brown University. Library. *Catalogue of Books in the Library of Brown University.* Providence: Printed at the Office of the Microcosm by Walter R. Danforth, 1826.

Charleston Library Society, Charleston, S.C. *A Catalogue of the Books Belonging to the Charleston Library Society.* Published by Order of the Society. Charleston: Printed by A. E. Miller, 1826.

Hamilton College, Clinton, N.Y. Library. *Catalogue of Hamilton College Library, January, 1826.* [n.p., n.d.]

Boston Athenaeum. *Catalogue of Books in the Boston Athenaeum: To Which Are Added the By-Laws of the Institution, and a List of Its Proprietors and Subscribers.* Boston: Printed by William L. Lewis, 1827.

Virginia. University. Library. *Catalogue of the Library of the University of Virginia. Arranged Alphabetically under Different Heads, with the Number and Size of the Volumes of Each Work, and Its Edition Specified. Also, a Notice of Such Donations of Books as Have Been Made to the University.* Charlottesville: Published by Gilmer, Davis & Co., 1828.

Pennsylvania. University. Library. *Catalogue of Books, Belonging to the Library of the University of Pennsylvania.* Philadelphia: J. Dobson, 1829.

Harvard University. Library. *A Catalogue of the Library of Harvard University in Cambridge, Massachusetts.* 3 vols. Cambridge: E. W. Metcalf & Co., 1830-31.

U.S. Library of Congress. *Catalogue of the Library of Congress. December, 1830.* Washington: Printed by Duff Green, 1830.

Philadelphia. Library Company. *A Catalogue of the Books Belonging to the Library Company of Philadelphia: To Which Is Prefixed, a Short Account of the Institution, with the Charter, Laws, and Regulations.* 2 vols. Philadelphia: C. Sherman & Co., Printers, 1835.

Vermont. University. Library. *Catalogue of the Books Belonging to the Library of the University of Vermont.* Burlington: V. Harrington, 1836.

Academy of Natural Sciences of Philadelphia. Library. *Catalogue of the Library of the Academy of Natural Sciences of Philadelphia.* Philadelphia: J. Dobson, 1837.

American Antiquarian Society, Worcester, Mass. *A Catalogue of Books in the Library of the American Antiquarian Society in Worcester, Massachusetts.* Worcester: Printed for the Society by Henry J. Howland, 1837.

Maryland. State Library. *Catalogue of the Library of the State of Maryland. D. Ridgely, Librarian. December, 1837.* Annapolis: Printed by Jeremiah Hughes, 1837.

New York. Mercantile Library Association. *Systematic Catalogue of Books in the Collection of the Mercantile Library Association of the City of New-York: With a General Index, and One of Dramatic Pieces, Together with an Appendix, Containing the Constitution, and the Rules and Regulations of the Association.* New-York: Printed by Harper & Bros., 1837.

Philadelphia. Library Company. Loganian Library. *Catalogue of the Books Belonging to the Loganian Library: To Which Is Prefixed a Short Account of the Institution, with the Law for Annexing the Said Library to That Belonging to "The Library Company of Philadelphia," and the Rules Regulating the Manner of Conducting the Same.* Philadelphia: C. Sherman & Co., Printers, 1837.

Providence, R.I. Athenaeum. *Catalogue of the Athenaeum Library: With an Appendix Containing the Library Regulations and a List of the Officers and Proprietors.* Providence: Knowles, Vose & Co., 1837.

Andover Theological Seminary. Library. *Catalogue of the Library of the Theol. Seminary in Andover, Mass.* By Oliver A. Taylor. Andover: Printed by Gould & Newman, 1838.

New York Society Library. *Alphabetical and Analytical Catalogue of the New-York Society Library: With a Brief Historical Notice of the Institution* ... New York: Printed by James Van Norden, 1838.

Philadelphia. Mercantile Library Company. *Catalogue of the*

*Books Belonging to the Mercantile Library Company of Phila-
delphia: With a General Index of Authors, And Containing the
Constitution, Rules, and Regulations of the Association. Accompanied by a Sketch of Its History.* Philadelphia: Printed
for the Company, 1840.

U.S. Library of Congress. *Catalogue of the Library of Congress,
in the Capitol of the United States of America, December,
1839.* City of Washington: Printed by Order of Congress,
1840.

Cincinnati. Young Men's Mercantile Library Association. *A Catalogue of Books Belonging to the Young Men's Mercantile Library Association of Cincinnati: To Which Are Prefixed the
Constitution, By-Laws, and Regulations of the Same.* Cincinnati: Printed by Shepard and Sterns, 1841.

Indiana State University. Library. *Catalogue of the Library of Indiana State University. Published by Order of the Board of
Trustees, 1842.* Bloomington: Printed by M. L. Deal, ₍1842₎.

Salem, Mass. Athenaeum. *Catalogue of the Library of the Athenaeum, in Salem, Massachusetts, with the By-Laws and Regulations.* Salem: Printed at the Office of the Gazette, 1842.

Brown University. Library. *A Catalogue of the Library of Brown
University, in Providence, Rhode Island. With an Index of
Subjects.* Providence: 1843.

Boston. Mercantile Library Association. *A Catalogue of Books of
the Boston Mercantile Library Association: Together with a
History of the Institution, Constitution, By-Laws, etc.* Boston:
Printed for the Association by Freeman & Bolles, 1844.

New York. Mercantile Library Association. *Catalogue of the
Mercantile Library in New York.* New York: Printed by
Edward O. Jenkins, 1844.

Cincinnati. Young Men's Mercantile Library. *Catalogue of the
Young Men's Mercantile Library, in Cincinnati.* Cincinnati:
Published by the Association, 1846.

Michigan. University. Library. *Catalogue of the Library of the
University of Michigan, 1846.* Ann Arbor: Printed by Order
of the Board of Regents, 1846.

Boston. Mercantile Library Association. *A Catalogue of Books of
the Mercantile Library Association, of Boston: Together with
the Act of Incorporation, and the By-Laws and Regulations,
Adopted January, 1848.* Boston: Printed for the Association,
1848.

Astor Library, New York. *Alphabetical Index of the Astor Li-
brary. Part I, Books Bought in 1849: To Which Is Prefixed a
Concise Classified Bibliography.* New York: R. Craighead,
Printer, 1849.

Pennsylvania Historical Society. Library. *Catalogue of the Library of the Historical Society of Pennsylvania. Part I, History, Biography and Manuscripts.* Philadelphia: Merrihew & Thompson, Printers, 1849.

South Carolina. University. Library. *Catalogue of the Library of the South Carolina College.* Columbia: Printed by A. S. Johnston, 1849.

U.S. Library of Congress. *Catalogue of the Library of Congress, June 30, 1849.* ₍Washington: 1849₎.

New York Society Library. *Alphabetical and Analytical Catalogue of the New York Society Library: With the Charter, By-Laws, etc. of the Institution.* New York: R. Craighead, Printer, 1850.

Philadelphia. Mercantile Library Company. *A Catalogue of the Mercantile Library Company of Philadelphia. Published April, 1850.* Philadelphia: Printed for the Company, 1850.

St. Louis. Mercantile Library Association. *Catalogue of Books Belonging to the St. Louis Mercantile Library Association, January, 1850.* St. Louis: The Association, 1850.

Astor Library, New York. *Alphabetical Index to the Astor Library, or Catalogue, with Short Titles, of the Books Now Collected and of the Proposed Accessions, as Submitted to the Trustees, Jan. 1851.* New York: R. Craighead, Printer, 1851.

Cambridge, Mass. High School. Library. *A Classed Catalogue of the Library of the Cambridge High School: With an Alphabetical Index. To Which Is Appended a List of the Philosophical and Other Apparatus Belonging to the School.* Cambridge: John Bartlett, 1853.

Providence, R.I. Athenaeum. *Catalogue of the Library of the Providence Athenaeum: To Which Are Prefixed the Charter, Constitution and By-Laws, and an Historical Sketch of the Institution.* Providence: Knowles, Anthony & Co., Printers, 1853.

Astor Library, New York. *Catalogue of Books ... Relating to the Languages and Literature of Asia, Africa, and the Oceanic Islands.* New York: Astor Library Autographic Pr., 1854.

Boston. Mercantile Library Association. *Catalogue of the Mercantile Library of Boston.* Boston: Printed by John Wilson & Son, 1854.

_____ Public Library. *Catalogue of the Public Library of the City of Boston ....* Boston: Printed by J. Wilson & Son, 1854.

Vermont. University. Library. *Alphabetical and Analytical Catalogue of the Library of the University of Vermont, Burlington.* Burlington: Free Press Off., 1854.

Amherst College. Library. *Catalogue of Amherst College Library.* Amherst: Printed by W. Faxon, 1855.

Cincinnati. Young Men's Mercantile Library Association. *Catalogue of the Young Men's Mercantile Library Association, of Cincinnati.* Cincinnati: Truman & Spofford, 1855.

General Society of Mechanics and Tradesmen of the City of New York. Library. *Catalogue of the Apprentices' and De Milt Libraries, New York...July 1, 1855.* New York: J. W. Amerman, Printer, 1855.

New York. Mercantile Library Association. *Catalogue of Books in the Mercantile Library of the City of New York. With a Supplement to August 1, 1856.* New York: Baker & Godwin, Printers, 1856.

Astor Library, New York. *Catalogue or Alphabetical Index of the Astor Library: In Two Parts. Part I, Authors and Books....* 4 vols. New York: R. Craighead, Printer, 1857-61.

Boston. Public Library. *Index to the Catalogue of a Portion of the Public Library of the City of Boston, Arranged in the Lower Hall....* Boston: Press of G. C. Rand & Avery, 1858.

Brooklyn. Mercantile Library Association. *A Catalogue of the Books in the Mercantile Library of the City of Brooklyn, N.Y., August, 1858.* Brooklyn: Printed by Baker & Godwin, 1858.

Massachusetts. State Library, Boston. *Catalogue of the State Library of Massachusetts.* Boston: W. White, Printer, 1858.

New Bedford, Mass. Free Public Library. *Catalogue of the Free Public Library, New Bedford, Mass.* New Bedford: B. Lindsey, Printer, 1858.

St. Louis. Mercantile Library Association. *Catalogue, Systematic and Analytical, of the Books of the Saint Louis Mercantile Library Association... by Edward W. Johnston, December, 1858.* St. Louis: Printed for the Association, 1858.

Pennsylvania. State Library. *Catalogue of the Pennsylvania State Library. Compiled and Classified by Wallace De Witt.* Harrisburg: A. B. Hamilton, State Printer, 1859.

California. State Library. *Catalogue of the California State Library. Prepared by W. C. Stratton.* Sacramento: C. T. Botts, State Printer, 1860.

Boston. Public Library. *Index to the Catalogue of Books in the Upper Hall of the Public Library of the City of Boston.* Boston: G. C. Rand & Avery, 1861.

Peabody Institute, Baltimore. Library. *Alphabetical Catalogue of Books Proposed To Be Purchased for the Library of the Peabody Institute, Baltimore.* Baltimore: Printed by J. D. Toy, 1861.

San Francisco. Mercantile Library Association. *A Classified*

Catalogue of the Mercantile Library of San Francisco, With an Index of Authors and Subjects, Consisting of about Fourteen Thousand Volumes. Made by the Librarian, January, 1861. San Francisco: Pub. by the Association, 1861.

U.S. Library of Congress. *Catalogue of the Library of Congress, Printed by Order of Congress.* Washington: L. Towers, Printer, 1861.

Bowdoin College. Library. *A Catalogue of the Library of Bowdoin College: To Which Is Added, an Index of Subjects.* Brunswick, ₜMaineₙ: Printed for the College, 1863.

Peabody Institute, Baltimore. Library. *Catalogue of Books To Be Purchased by the Peabody Institute of the City of Baltimore.* Baltimore: Printed by J. D. Toy, 1863.

U.S. Library of Congress. *Alphabetical Catalogue of the Library of Congress: Authors.* Washington: Govt. Print. Off., 1864.

General Society of Mechanics and Tradesmen of the City of New York. Library. *Catalogue of the Apprentices' Library in New-York. Established and Supported by the General Society of Mechanics and Tradesmen, September, 1865.* New York: A. W. King, Printer, 1865.

New York. Mercantile Library Association. *Catalogue of Books in the Mercantile Library, of the City of New York. . . .* New York: F. T. Taylor, Printer, 1866.

Dartmouth College. Library. *A Catalogue of the Library of Dartmouth College.* Hanover: Printed at the Dartmouth Pr., 1868.

Detroit. Public Library. *Catalogue of the Public Library of the City of Detroit, Containing an Alphabetical List of the Names of Authors, with the Titles of Their Works, and of the Titles of Anonymous Works Whose Authors Are Unknown. Also the Rules Concerning Its Use.* Detroit: Advertiser & Tribune Print. Co., 1868.

Cincinnati. Young Men's Mercantile Library Association. *Catalogue of the Books of the Young Men's Mercantile Library Association of Cincinnati.* Cincinnati: 1869.

U.S. Library of Congress. *Catalogue of the Library of Congress: Index of Subjects.* 2 vols. Washington: Govt. Print. Off., 1869.

Philadelphia. Mercantile Library Company. *Catalogue of the Mercantile Library of Philadelphia.* Philadelphia: Mercantile Library Company, 1870.

St. Louis. Public School Library. *Catalogue, Classified and Alphabetical, of the Books of the St. Louis Public School Library: Including, also, the Collections of the St. Louis Academy of Science, and St. Louis Law School. Prepared, under the Direction of the Board of Managers, by Jno. Jay Bailey,*

Librarian. St. Louis: Missouri Democrat Book and Job Print. House, 1870.

Waterbury, Conn. Silas Bronson Library. *Catalogue of the Silas Bronson Library of the City of Waterbury, Conn.* Waterbury: Press of the American Print. Co., 1870.

Cincinnati. Public Library. *Catalogue of the Public Library of Cincinnati.* Cincinnati: Press of Wilstach, Baldwin & Co., 1871.

Minnesota. University. Library. *An Alphabetical Catalogue of Authors. Complete to March 31, 1872.* St. Paul: Ramaley, Chaney & Co., Printers, 1872.

U.S. Surgeon-General's Office. *Catalogue of the Library of the Surgeon-General's Office, United States Army. With an Alphabetical Index of Subjects.* Washington: Govt. Print. Off., 1872.

Boston. Public Library. *A Catalogue of Books Belonging to the Lower Hall of the Central Department, in the Classes of History, Biography, and Travel, Including the Histories of Literature, Art, Sects, etc., Politics, Geography, Voyages, Sketches, and Manners and Customs: Together with Notes for Readers under Subject-References.* 2d or consolidated ed., July, 1873. Boston: Issued by the Library, 1873.

Indianapolis. Public Library. *Catalogue of the Public Library of Indianapolis, 1873.* Indianapolis: Press of Print. and Pub. House, 1873.

U.S. Surgeon-General's Office. *Catalogue of the Library of the Surgeon-General's Office, United States Army. . . .* 3 vols. Washington: Govt. Print. Off., 1873-74.

Wisconsin. State Historical Society. Library. *Catalogue of the Library of the State Historical Society of Wisconsin. Prepared by Daniel S. Durrie, Librarian, and Isabel Durrie, Assistant.* 7 vols. Madison: Pub. by Order of the State, 1873-87.

Boston Athenaeum. *Catalogue of the Library of the Boston Athenaeum, 1807-1871.* 5 vols. Boston: 1874-82.

Chicago. Public Library. *Temporary Finding Lists for Alcoves A. to L., July, 1874.* ₍n.p., n.d.₎

Columbia University. Library. *Catalogue of the Books and Pamphlets in the Library of Columbia College, New York. Printed for the Trustees.* New York: J. W. Amerman, Printer, 1874.

General Society of Mechanics and Tradesmen of the City of New York. Library. *Catalogue of the Apprentices' Library, Established and Supported by the General Society of Mechanics and Tradesmen of the City of New York. . . . With a Supplement of Additions and Omissions, and a Special Catalogue of Prose*

Fiction and Juvenile Literature. Comp. by J. Schwartz, Jr., Librarian, September, 1874. New York: Chatterton & Parker, Printers, 1874.

St. Louis. Mercantile Library Association. *Classified Catalogue of the Saint Louis Mercantile Library, with Index of Authors.* St. Louis: Printed for the Association by the Democrat Lithograph. and Print. Co., 1874.

San Francisco. Mercantile Library Association. *Catalogue of the Library of the Mercantile Library Association of San Francisco. Pub. by the Association.* San Francisco: Francis & Valentine, Printers, 1874.

Chicago. Public Library. *Temporary Finding Lists, February, 1875.* 2d ed. Chicago: Hazlitt & Reed, Printers, 1875.

Quincy, Mass. Public Library. *Catalogue of the Public Library of Quincy, Mass.* Boston: Press of Rockwell & Churchill, 1875.

Williams College, Williamstown, Mass. Library. *Catalogue of the Library of Williams College, Williamstown, Mass., 1875.* North Adams: J. T. Robinson & Son, Printers and Binders, 1875.

Charleston Library Society, Charleston, S.C. *Catalogue of the Books Belonging to the Charleston Library Society. Published by Order of the Society.* Charleston: News and Courier Book and Job Pr., 1876.

Chicago. Public Library. *Finding Lists of the Chicago Public Library.* 3d ed. Chicago: Printed by Jefferson & Wroe, 1876.

Cincinnati. Public Library. *Catalogue of Books in English, French and German, Belonging to the Class of Prose Fiction, in the Public Library of Cincinnati.* Cincinnati: Pub. by the Board of Managers, 1876.

Galesburg, Ill. Public Library. *Catalogue of Books Contained in the Galesburg Public Library and Reading Room, January 1, 1876.* Galesburg: Printed by the Galesburg Print. Co., 1876.

New York. Mercantile Library Association. *Catalogue of English Prose Fiction, in the Mercantile Library of the City of New York, to July, 1876. Published by the Association.* New York: Allen & Co., Stationers and Printers, 1876.

Brooklyn Library. *Catalogue of the Mercantile Library of Brooklyn: Authors, Titles, Subjects, and Classes.* Brooklyn, N.Y.: 1877-80.

Detroit. Public Library. *Catalogue of the Public Library of the City of Detroit, 1877.* Detroit: Detroit Print. Co., 1877.

New York. City College. Library. *Catalogue of the Library of the College of the City of New York.* 2 vols. New York: 1877-78.

Haverhill, Mass. Public Library. *Catalogue of the Public Library of Haverhill.* Haverhill: Press of Franklin P. Stiles, 1878.

U.S. Library of Congress. *Alphabetical Catalogue of the Library of Congress.* 2 vols. (A-Cragin.) Washington: Govt. Print. Off., 1878-80.

Cleveland. Public Library. *Classified Catalogue of Cleveland Public Library.* Cleveland: 1879.

Massachusetts. State Library. *Catalogue of the State Library of Massachusetts.* Boston: Rand, Avery & Co., 1880.

San Francisco. Public Library. *Catalogue of the San Francisco Free Public Library... Short Titles.* 3 vols. San Francisco: The Library, ₍1880-82₎.

U.S. Surgeon-General's Office. *Index-Catalogue of the Library of the Surgeon-General's Office, United States Army: Authors and Subjects....* 16 vols. Washington: Govt. Print. Off., 1880-95.

Minnesota. University. Library. *Finding Lists of the Library of the University of Minnesota. Complete to September, 1881.* 1st ed. St. Paul: J. K. Moore, 1881.

Fall River, Mass. Public Library. *Catalogue of the Public Library of the City of Fall River.* Fall River: Press of Fiske & Munroe, 1882.

Peabody Institute, Baltimore. Library. *Catalogue of the Library of the Peabody Institute of the City of Baltimore.* 5 vols. Baltimore: ₍I. Friedenwald₎, 1883-92.

Dayton, Ohio. Public Library. *Catalogue of the Dayton Public Library: Authors, Subjects, and Titles. Published by the Board of Education.* Dayton: United Brethren Pub. House, 1884.

Princeton University. Library. *Subject-Catalogue of the Library of the College of New Jersey, at Princeton.* New York: ₍C. M. Green Print. Co.₎, 1884.

Worcester, Mass. Free Public Library. *Catalogue of the Circulating Department, and a Portion of the Books Belonging to the Intermediate Department. Worcester, 1884.* Worcester: Printed by C. Hamilton, 1884.

Danville, Ill. Public Library. *Catalogue of the Danville Public Library and Reading Room.* 2d ed. Danville: Illinois Print. Co., 1885.

Indianapolis. Public Library. *Alphabetic Catalogue of the Indianapolis Public Library, 1885: Authors, Titles and Subjects.* Indianapolis: Carlon & Hollenbeck, Printers, 1885.

Milwaukee. Public Library. *Systematic Catalogue of the Public Library of the City of Milwaukee: With Alphabetical Author, Title, and Subject Indexes. 1885.* Milwaukee: Published by the Board of Trustees of the Library, 1885-86.

Astor Library, New York. *Catalogue of the Astor Library (Continuation): Authors and Books.* 4 vols. Cambridge, ₍Mass.₎: Printed at the Riverside Pr., 1886-88.

Fitchburg, Mass. Public Library. *Classified Catalogue of the Public Library, of Fitchburg, Mass., Comprising Author and Title Catalogue, Subject Catalogue, and Subject Index.* Compiled by George Watson Cole. Fitchburg: Press of Blanchard & Brown, 1886.

Harvard University. Library. *Index to the Subject Catalogue of Harvard College Library.* Cambridge, Mass.: Library of Harvard University, 1886-91.

Galesburg, Ill. Public Library. *Finding List of the Galesburg Public Library, 1887.* Galesburg: Press of Colville & Bro., ₍1887₎.

California. State Library. *Catalogue of the California State Library, General Department: Authors. By Talbot H. Wallis, State Librarian.* Sacramento: J. D. Young, Superintendent of State Printing, 1889.

———— University. Library. *Contents-Index, Vol. 1.* Berkeley: 1889-90.

Detroit. Public Library. *General Catalogue of the Books, Except Fiction, French, and German, in the Public Library of Detroit, Mich., 1888.* Detroit: O. S. Gulley, Bornman & Co., 1889.

Minneapolis. Public Library. *Finding List of English Prose Fiction, and Books for the Young: Author, Title and Topic. November, 1890.* Minneapolis: Tribune Job Print. Co., ₍1890₎.

Jersey City, N.J. Public Library. *Alphabetical Finding List of the Free Public Library of Jersey City, N.J., August 1, 1891.* Jersey City: Jersey City Print. Co., 1891.

Los Angeles. Public Library. *Finding List of Books in the Los Angeles Public Library, January, 1891.* Los Angeles: Times-Mirror Print. and Bind. House, 1891.

Philadelphia. Mercantile Library Company. *Alphabetical List (by Title) of the Class of Prose Fiction in the Mercantile Library of Philadelphia.* Philadelphia: Printed for the Library, 1891.

San Francisco. Public Library. *Classified English Prose Fiction: Including Translations and Juvenile Works with Notes and Index to Subject-References.* San Francisco: H. S. Crocker Co., Printers, 1891.

Evanston, Ill. Public Library. *Finding List of the Free Public Library of the City of Evanston, Ill., July, 1892.* Evanston: Index Co., Printers, ₍1892₎.

New London, Conn. Public Library. *Finding-List of the Public*

Library of New London. ... January, 1892. New York: Rapid Print Co., 1892.

St. Louis. Mercantile Library Association. *Catalogue of the St. Louis Mercantile Library. Section I, English Prose Fiction.* ...St. Louis: Nixon-Jones Print. Co., 1892.

Bloomington, Ill. Withers Public Library. *Finding List, November, 1894*. Bloomington: J. E. Burke & Co., Printers, 1894.

Decatur, Ill. Public Library. *Catalogue of the Free Public Library, of Decatur, Ill.* Decatur: Herald-Despatch Co., 1894.

Peoria, Ill. Public Library. *List of English Fiction, French Fiction, and Juveniles. Arranged Alphabetically by Author and Title. May, 1894*. Peoria: Press of H. S. Hill Print. Co., 1894.

Utica, N.Y. Public Library. *Finding List, May, 1895*. Utica: L. C. Childs & Son, 1895.

Peabody Institute, Baltimore. Library. *Second Catalogue of the Library of the Peabody Institute of the City of Baltimore: Including the Additions Made Since 1882*. 8 vols. Baltimore: 1896-1905.

Mattoon, Ill. Public Library. *Finding List of the Free Public Library, Mattoon, Illinois. June 1, 1897*. Mattoon: Mattoon Commercial Print., 1897.

St. Louis. Public Library. *English Prose Fiction, 1897: Class List No. 1*. St. Louis: Published by the Library, 1897.

Pittsburgh. Carnegie Library. *Classified Catalogue of the Carnegie Library of Pittsburgh*. Series I-IV. 11 vols. Pittsburgh: Carnegie Library, 1907-26.

BOOKS AND PERIODICALS

Only those sources found to be most useful are included.

"A.L.A. Catalog," *Library Journal*, 4:123 (Apr., 1879).

Abbot, Ezra. "Mr. Abbot's Statement Respecting the New Catalogues of the College Library," Harvard University, *Report of the Committee of the Overseers of Harvard College Appointed To Visit the Library for the Year 1863: Together with the Accompanying Documents. Submitted January 28, 1864*, p.35-68. Boston: 1864.

American Library Association. Committee on Publishers' Title-Slips. "Report of Committee on Title-Slips," *Library Journal*, 3:113-15 (May, 1878).

Baker, Maysel O. "American Library Catalogs a Hundred Years Ago," *Wilson Library Bulletin*, 33:284-85, 291 (Dec., 1958).

Besterman, Theodore. *The Beginnings of Systematic Bibliography.* 2d ed., rev. London: Oxford Univ. Pr., 1936.

Billstein, Nathan. "Linotyping Library Catalogs — Pro and Con," *Library Journal,* 19:257-58 (Aug., 1894).

Bishop, William Warner. "Margaret Mann," *Catalogers' and Classifiers' Yearbook,* 7:11-14 (1938).

Borome, Joseph Alfred. *Charles Coffin Jewett.* ("American Library Pioneers," VII.) Chicago: American Library Association, 1951.

Boston Athenaeum. *The Athenaeum Centenary: The Influence and History of the Boston Athenaeum from 1807 to 1907....* Boston: Boston Athenaeum, 1907.

Brough, Kenneth J. *Scholar's Workshop: Evolving Conceptions of Library Service.* ("Illinois Contributions to Librarianship," No. 5.) Urbana: Univ. of Illinois Pr., 1953.

Brubacher, John Seiler, and Rudy, Willis. *Higher Education in Transition: An American History, 1636-1956.* New York: Harper, 1958.

"Central Card Cataloging," *Library Journal,* 18:508-10 (Dec., 1893).

Cranage, David Herbert Somerset. *The Home of the Monk: An Account of English Monastic Life and Buildings in the Middle Ages.* Cambridge, Eng.: Univ. Pr., 1926.

Crunden, Frederick M. "Report on Aids and Guides," *Library Journal,* 11:309-30 (Milwaukee Conference Number, 1886).

Cutter, Charles Ammi. "The Athenaeum Catalogue," *Library Journal,* 3:191-92 (July, 1878).

_____ "The Cataloguer's Work," *The Nation,* 24:86-88 (Feb. 8, 1877).

_____ "The Editor to the Proprietors," Boston Athenaeum, *Catalogue of the Library of the Boston Athenaeum, 1807-1871,* 5: 3399-402. Boston: 1874-82.

_____ *Expansive Classification, Part I: The First Six Classifications.* Boston: C. A. Cutter, 1891-93.

_____ "Library Catalogues," U.S. Bureau of Education, *Public Libraries in the United States of America: Their History, Condition, and Management.* Special Report, Part I, p.526-622. Washington: Govt. Print. Off., 1876.

_____ "The New Catalogue of Harvard College Library," *North American Review,* 108:96-129 (Jan., 1869).

Dewey, Melvil. *A Classification and Subject Index for Cataloguing and Arranging the Books and Pamphlets of a Library.* Amherst, Mass.: 1876.

_____ "The Coming Catalogue," *Library Journal,* 1:423-27 (Aug., 1877).

_____ "A Decimal Classification and Subject Index," U.S. Bureau of Education, *Public Libraries in the United States of America: Their History, Condition, and Management.* Special Report, Part I, p.623-48. Washington: Govt. Print. Off., 1876.

_____ "Public Documents," *Library Journal,* 1:10-11 (Sept., 1876).

Dury, John. *The Reformed Librarie-Keeper: or, Two Copies of Letters Concerning the Place and Office of a Librarie-Keeper.* ("Literature of Libraries in the Seventeenth and Eighteenth Centuries," J. C. Dana and H. W. Kent, eds.) Chicago: A. C. McClurg, 1906.

Edwards, Edward. *Memoirs of Libraries: Including a Handbook of Library Economy.* 2 vols. London: Truebner, 1859.

Fletcher, William I. "Annotation," *Library Journal,* 29:144-47 (St. Louis Conference Number, 1904).

_____ "The Future of the Catalog," *Library Journal,* 30:141-44 (Mar., 1905).

_____ *Public Libraries in America.* Boston: Roberts Bros., 1894.

Flint, Weston. *Statistics of Public Libraries in the United States and Canada.* ("U.S. Bureau of Education, Circular of Information," No. 7, 1893.) Washington: Govt. Print. Off., 1893.

"General Statistics of All Public Libraries in the United States," U.S. Bureau of Education, *Public Libraries in the United States of America: Their History, Condition, and Management.* Special Report, Part I, p.1010-1174. Washington: Govt. Print. Off., 1876.

Goldberg, Arthur. *The Buffalo Public Library: Commemorating Its First Century of Service to the Citizens of Buffalo, 1836-1936.* Buffalo, N.Y.: Privately printed, 1937.

Green, Samuel Swett. "Report of the Committee on the Distribution of Public Documents," *Library Journal,* 6:86-90 (Washington Conference Number, 1881).

Hagen, H. A. "The Librarian's Work," *The Nation,* 24:40-41 (Jan. 18, 1877).

Harris, William T. "Essay on the System of Classification," St. Louis, Public School Library, *Catalogue: Classified and Alphabetical . . .,* p.ix-xvi. St. Louis: Missouri Democrat Book and Job Print. House, 1870.

Hessel, Alfred. *A History of Libraries;* tr., with supplementary material, by Reuben Peiss. Washington, D.C.: Scarecrow Pr., 1950.

Homes, Henry A. "Historical Societies in the United States," U.S. Bureau of Education, *Public Libraries in the United States of America: Their History, Condition, and Management.* Special Report, Part I, p.312-24. Washington: Govt. Print. Off., 1876.

_____ "State and Territorial Libraries," *ibid.*, p.292-311.

Jayne, Sears. *Library Catalogues of the English Renaissance.* Berkeley: Univ. of California Pr., 1956.

Jewett, Charles Coffin. *Appendix to the Report of the Board of Regents of the Smithsonian Institution, Containing a Report on the Public Libraries, January 1, 1850.* (31st Cong., 1st Sess., House Miscellaneous, No. 50.) Washington: Printed for the House of Reps., 1850.

_____ ...*On the Construction of Catalogues of Libraries, and Their Publication by Means of Separate, Stereotyped Titles, with Rules and Examples.* Smithsonian Report. 2d ed. Washington: Smithsonian Institution, 1853.

_____ "Second Report of the Assistant Secretary of the Smithsonian Institution, Relative to the Library — Presented Jan. 2, 1850," *Fourth Annual Report of the Board of Regents of the Smithsonian Institution...during the Year 1849.* (31st Cong., 1st Sess., House Miscellaneous, No. 50.) Washington: Printed by the Printers to the House of Reps., 1850.

Keep, Austin Baxter. *History of the New York Society Library.* New York: De Vinne Pr., 1908.

Kenyon, Frederic George. *Books and Readers in Ancient Greece and Rome.* Oxford: Clarendon Pr., 1932.

Kramer, Samuel Noah. *From the Tablets of Sumer.* Indian Hills, Colo.: Falcon's Wing Pr., 1956.

Lane, William C. "Cataloging," in Melvil Dewey, ed., *Papers Prepared for the World's Library Congress Held at the Columbian Exposition,* p.835-49. Washington: Govt. Print. Off., 1896.

_____ "Report of the A.L.A. Publishing Section," *Library Journal,* 22:84-86 (Philadelphia Conference Number, 1897).

_____ "Report on Catalogues and Aids and Guides for Readers, 1885-87," *Library Journal,* 12:414-22 (Thousand Islands Conference Number, 1887).

"Linotyping Library Catalogs: A Symposium," *Library Journal,* 19:259-61 (Aug., 1894).

McKerrow, Ronald B. *An Introduction to Bibliography for Literary Students.* Oxford: Clarendon Pr., 1949.

McMurtrie, Douglas C. *The Book: The Story of Printing and Bookmaking.* 3d rev. ed. New York: Oxford Univ. Pr., 1943.

Martel, Charles. "The Newberry Blue-Print Catalog," *Library Journal,* 24:608 (Nov., 1899).

Mengel, Willi. *Ottmar Mergenthaler and the Printing Revolution: With an Introduction by Lin Yutang.* Brooklyn: Mergenthaler Linotype Co., 1954.

Morison, Samuel Eliot. *The Intellectual Life of Colonial New England.* 2d ed. New York: New York Univ. Pr., 1956.

Nelson, Charles A. "Publishers' Slips for Librarians and Others," *Library Journal,* 1:15 (Sept., 1876).

"The Newberry Blue-Print Catalog," *Library Journal,* 24:574 (Oct., 1899).

Norris, Dorothy May. *A History of Cataloguing and Cataloguing Methods, 1100-1850: With an Introductory Survey of Ancient Times.* London: Grafton, 1939.

Noyes, Stephen B. "Cataloguing," *Library Journal,* 8:166-72 (Buffalo Conference Number, 1883).

_____ "Plan of New Catalogue of the Brooklyn Mercantile Library," U.S. Bureau of Education, *Public Libraries in the United States of America: Their History, Condition, and Management.* Special Report, Part I, p.648-56. Washington: Govt. Print. Off., 1876.

Panizzi, Anthony. "Rules for the Compilation of the Catalogue," British Museum, Department of Printed Books, *Catalogue of Printed Books in the British Museum. Volume I,* p.v-ix. London: 1841.

Perkins, Frederic B. "Young Men's Mercantile Libraries," U.S. Bureau of Education, *Public Libraries in the United States of America: Their History, Condition, and Management.* Special Report, Part I, p.378-85. Washington: Govt. Print. Off., 1876.

Pinner, H. L. *The World of Books in Classical Antiquity.* Leiden: A. W. Sijthoff, 1948.

"The Plan of the New 'Poole's Index': A Library Symposium," *Library Journal,* 3:141-51 (June, 1878).

Poole, William F. "The Organization and Management of Public Libraries," U.S. Bureau of Education, *Public Libraries in the United States of America: Their History, Condition, and Management.* Special Report, Part I, p.476-504. Washington: Govt. Print. Off., 1876.

_____ "The Plan of the New 'Poole's Index,'" *Library Journal,* 3:109-10 (May, 1878).

Predeek, Albert. *A History of Libraries in Great Britain and North America;* tr. by Lawrence S. Thompson. Chicago: American Library Association, 1947.

"Public, Society, and School Libraries," U.S. Bureau of Education, *Report of the Commissioner of Education for the Year Ending June 30, 1900.* Volume I, p.923-1165. (56th Cong., 2d Sess., House of Representatives, Document No. 5.) Washington: Govt. Print. Off., 1901.

"Publication Section: Printed Catalog Cards," *Library Journal,*
    12:515 (Nov., 1887).
Richardson, Ernest C. "The Linotype Method," *Library Journal,*
    17:377-78 (Sept., 1892).
_____ "Report of the Co-operation Committee," *Library Journal,*
    25:71-73 (Montreal Conference Number, 1900).
Robinson, Otis H. "College Library Administration," U.S. Bureau
    of Education, *Public Libraries in the United States of Amer-
    ica: Their History, Condition, and Management.* Special Re-
    port, Part I, p.505-25. Washington: Govt. Print. Off., 1876.
Rudolph, Alexander J. "The Blue-Print Process for Printing Cat-
    alogs," *Library Journal,* 24:102-5 (Mar., 1899).
Schley, Ruth. "Cataloging in the Libraries of Princeton, Columbia,
    and the University of Pennsylvania before 1876." Unpublished
    master's thesis, School of Library Service, Columbia Univ.,
    1946.
Schwartz, Jacob. "New York Apprentices' Library Catalogue,"
    U.S. Bureau of Education, *Public Libraries in the United
    States of America: Their History, Condition, and Manage-
    ment.* Special Report, Part I, p.657-60. Washington: Govt.
    Print. Off., 1876.
Shera, Jesse Hauk. *Foundations of the Public Library: The Ori-
    gins of the Public Library Movement in New England, 1629-
    1855.* Chicago: Univ. of Chicago Pr., 1949.
Shores, Louis. *Origins of the American College Library, 1638-
    1800.* New York: Barnes & Noble, 1935.
Storie, Catharine P. "What Contribution Did the American College
    Society Library Make to the College Library? A Supplemen-
    tary Chapter in the History of the American College Library."
    Unpublished master's thesis, School of Library Service, Co-
    lumbia Univ., 1938.
Strout, Ruth French. "The Development of the Catalog and Cata-
    loging Codes," *Library Quarterly,* 26:254-75 (Oct., 1956).
Taylor, Archer. *Book Catalogues: Their Varieties and Uses.* Chi-
    cago: Newberry Library, 1957.
Thompson, Charles Seymour. *Evolution of the American Public
    Library, 1653-1876.* Washington, D.C.: Scarecrow Pr., 1952.
Thompson, James Westfall. *The Medieval Library.* Chicago:
    Univ. of Chicago Pr., 1939.
Utley, George Burwell. *The Librarians' Conference of 1853: A
    Chapter in American Library History,* Gilbert H. Doane, ed.
    Chicago: American Library Association, 1951.
Whitney, James Lyman. "Considerations as to a Printed Catalogue
    in Book Form," Boston Public Library, *Forty-Seventh Annual
    Report... 1898,* p.49-59.

Winsor, Justin. "The College Library," U.S. Bureau of Education, *College Libraries as Aids of Instruction,* p.7-14. ("Circulars of Information," No. 1, 1880.) Washington: Govt. Print. Off., 1880.

Wire, George E. "Report on Classification and Cataloging," *Library Journal,* 23:18-22 (Chautauqua Conference Number, 1898).

Wright, Louis Booker. *The Cultural Life of the American Colonies, 1607-1763.* ("The New American Nation Series.") New York: Harper, 1957.

Wright, Thomas Goddard. *Literary Culture in Early New England, 1620-1730,* ed. by his wife. New Haven: Yale Univ. Pr., 1920.

Index